5,45

RACQUETBALL

Bill Verner
with
Drew Skowrup

 Mayfield Publishing Company

Copyright © 1977 by Bill Verner
First edition, 1977

Library of Congress Catalog Card Number: 77-089923
International Standard Book Number: 0-87484-426-6

Manufactured in the United States of America
Mayfield Publishing Company
285 Hamilton Avenue, Palo Alto, California 94301

This book was set in Melior by Chapman's Phototypesetting an
was printed and bound by National Press. Sponsoring editor w
C. Lansing Hays, Carole Norton supervised editing, and Ma
Winitz was manuscript editor. Michelle Hogan supervised pr
duction, and the book and cover were designed by Nancy Sear

CONTENTS

61641

PREFACE

Today's sports and recreation enthusiasts are making racquetball the fastest growing participation sport in America. Courts and clubs are springing up everywhere and rapidly becoming as popular as traditional golf courses and tennis courts. Players are flocking to private clubs, YMCA's, and high school and college physical education classes to learn and participate.

Once you've played racquetball, you'll know why millions are drawn to this stimulating game. While many racket sports take years to perfect and learn, the basics of racquetball can be taught in fifteen minutes. Even those unaccustomed to sports can acquire racquetball skills easily and rapidly.

If you're promoting physical and mental health, you'll find few routes as quick and direct as racquetball. The enclosed court makes it possible to spend more time playing and less effort retrieving balls, than in other sports. An hour on the court, a few times a week, will strengthen the heart and increase general cardio-vascular fitness, as well as tone and firm up muscles. You will also find that a casual game with a friend can do wonders to release built-up tensions. Whatever your present athletic ability or level of fitness, you will discover that racquetball is an excellent activity for getting and keeping in shape.

But the most important reason for racquetball's phenomenal popularity is simply that the game is fun! Because its skills are so easily learned, everyone—men, women, teenagers, and children—can enjoy racquetball the first time on the court. Both the beginner and the more advanced player will find this book designed to add enjoyment and knowledge to the sport. Racquetball can be played for a lifetime, and it is a sport for everyone. Try it just once and you'll see why.

HISTORY

The foundations of modern racquetball, as well as almost all other court sports, were built more than seven centuries ago. Its beginnings can be traced to a game played by French noblemen and ladies who used their hands to bat a cloth bag over a net. Later, gloves, bats, paddles, and eventually rackets were used, and the game of court tennis was devised.

Although racquetball claims its early origins in court tennis, it evolved more directly from the game of paddleball. Paddleball is a cross between handball and tennis, and was first played on handball courts at the University of Michigan in the 1920's. The popularity of paddleball grew when the game was selected as one of the activities of the United States armed forces conditioning program held at the university.

In the 1940's, a racquet strung with gut strings was introduced to paddleball as an alternative to the solid wooden type. The original name of this new game which required a racquet with strings was "paddle-rackets." The early rules for the game were derived primarily from established squash and handball rules. As the popularity of "paddle rackets" grew, especially toward the 1960's, national tournaments were started. The first international championships were conducted in 1969, in St. Louis, Mo. At this tournament an organization meeting was held and the International Racquetball Association (I.R.A.) was established. In addition, the name of the game was officially changed from "paddle rackets" to racquetball. The Association also stressed the spelling of "racquet," rather than "racket." During the meeting Robert Kendler, former presi-

dent and founder of the United States Handball Association, assumed the role of president of the I.R.A.

In the early developmental stages of the International Racquetball Association, authority and organization were handled primarily by the United States Handball Association, which provided publicity for the new game in their handball magazine. Soon, however, there arose a severe conflict between the old handball players and the new racquetball enthusiasts. There was a tremendous lack of handball courts across the country, and the promotion of a new sport which used these already overcrowded facilities magnified the hostility among handball players. As a result of this problem, racquetball was banned in many YMCAs and private clubs, where most of the handball courts were located. It soon became evident that the solution was not in limiting the play of racquetball, but in developing more facilities. This would allow the two games to grow separately from each other, rather than in opposition.

As racquetball began to develop it was soon able to publish its own magazine, apart from the handball magazine. This was a turning point which signified that racquetball had survived on its own, and could be supported by its own membership.

In 1973, during their yearly meeting, Kendler resigned as president of the I.R.A. and formed a rival organization, known as the National Racquetball Club (N.R.C.) This group now sponsors a professional tour for the top players in the country, and also plays father to an organization for amateur players, called the United States Racquetball Association (U.S.R.A.).

Innovations in equipment and facilities have been rapid during the short history of the game. The heavy, wood framed racquets were soon made of aluminum, fiberglass, carbon composition, and mixtures of plastic and fiberglass. They became lighter, easier to swing, and they were strung looser for more control over a livelier ball.

The only balls which were suitable for play in the early stages of racquetball were tennis balls. Today, after several stages of evolution, highly pressurized balls are used, which makes the four-wall game speedier and more lively. The courts have changed, also—from all concrete walls to some with glass sidewalls and backwalls for better viewing. Superior floor and wall textures, as well as improved lighting and seating arrangements, have made racquetball more enjoyable for both players and spectators.

The growth of racquetball has been phenomenal, and the game is still expanding. For example, just a few years ago manufacturers were producing only ten thousand racquets a year. Today this number is produced every week. Although racquetball sports a relatively short history, it promises an enormous future.

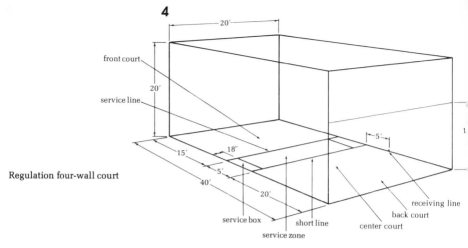

4

Regulation four-wall court

PRE-GAME BASICS

Types of courts

Racquetball can be played on one-, three-, or four-wall courts. The most popular is the enclosed, four-wall court with a ceiling. However, at the junior and senior high school levels one- and three-wall courts are more common than the more expensive four-wall style.

This book deals mainly with four-wall play, but most of the principles you will learn here can also be used on one- and three-walls.

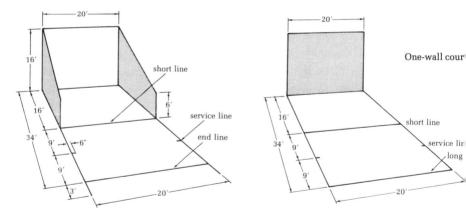

Popular three-wall court

One-wall court

The walls of racquetball courts may be made from various materials, including cement, and prefabricated fiber-resin panels. Four-wall courts may be constructed of glass, for better viewing by spectators. Official indoor courts have wooden floors, although schools often select cement, as a less expensive alternative.

Basic rules

Racquetball can be played with two (singles), three (cut-throat), or four players (doubles). Singles and doubles are used in club and tournament competition. In cutthroat, the server is always playing against the two receivers. When the server loses the rally, another player earns the serve and he plays against the two receivers. Although cutthroat is not allowed in tournament play, it is often seen in racquetball clubs and on school courts.

To start the game, the server stands in the service area, bounces the ball, and strikes it so it hits the front wall and rebounds into the court anywhere beyond the short line. On the serve, the ball may hit only one side wall and must strike the front wall first. A serve which hits the front wall, and then either the back wall or ceiling, is a fault, and is replayed. Serves which hit two side walls or do not travel beyond the short line are also faults, and are replayed. If a served ball hits any other surface before it strikes the front wall, the server loses his serve.

After the ball passes the short line, the receiver must return the ball to the front wall before it bounces on the floor twice. Unlike the serve, the return may hit any wall first, as long as it eventually hits the front wall before the second bounce. After service, the players hit the ball alternately. The ball may be hit in the air before it bounces; however, it must be hit and returned to the front wall before it bounces twice. Additionally, the ball can take any route to the front wall, hitting the ceiling, front and side walls in any combination.

Scoring

Only the server, or serving team, can score points. If the receiver wins the rally, he gains only the serve, and with it his own opportunity to score. The game ends when one player, or team, scores 21 points. There is no deuce game, overtime, or win-by-two points rule, as in ping-pong or tennis. The game ends at 21 points, even if the score is 21-20. A match usually consists of three games; the player, or team, which wins two of them is considered the winner. Professional tournaments limit the third game to 11 points, but this rule is currently being challenged, and may change in the future.

At the present time, a new scoring system is being used by many clubs. All games are played to 15, but the first player who reaches 15 points must be ahead by at least two points. If the score is 15-14, for example, play is continued until a player has a two-point advantage, and then the game ends. If the score reaches 20-20, the player winning the next point automatically wins the game.

Safety hinders

Since racquetball is played in a confined area certain precautions should be undertaken. *You should always stop*

your swing if there is any possibility of hitting your opp
nent with the racquet or ball. In all cases that might resu
in an injury, the word "hinder" should be called out, an
the rally replayed. This is an unwritten hinder rule th
should be followed diligently. Additional hinder rule
which are written into the regulations, should be learne
before beginning play.

Etiquette

One of the most important things to remember when yc
are playing racquetball is that the game is meant for enjo
ment. Most players value the experience of participatio:
the exercise, and the pleasure of making an occasion
great shot. Observing the courtesies of court etiquette n
only makes the game more enjoyable, it also helps mal
the game safer. Remember the following pointers whi
playing racquetball:

1 Good sportsmanship is the foundation of racquetba
etiquette. Treat others as you would like to be treate

2 Show up on time for your match.

3 Greet your opponent and introduce yourself.

4 Your warm-up period should not exceed 5 minute
Don't warm up for half an hour. On the other hand, do
rush your opponent to begin the game.

5 Wait until your opponent is ready before serving.

6 Call out the score (server's score first) before each ser
This will help avoid confusion and argument, and t
game will continue smoothly.

7 Don't be a wild swinger on the court. Over swinging c
cause injuries.

8 Talk only when necessary during the match, nev
while your opponent is making a shot. However, a
knowledge a good shot by your opponent. In double
it is permissible to help your partner by calling for c
tain shots.

9 Control your temper. Banging your racquet agai
walls and floor is expensive and dangerous.

10 Be fair on your calls and shots. If your shot "skips i
and your opponent does not see it, call it against yo
self. Fair play leads to friendship on and off the cou

11 Give your opponent a fair chance to return the ba
Don't intentionally block his view.

12 Don't crowd or push your opponent. The closer you g
to him/her, the greater the chances are of getting h
either with the ball, or the racquet.

13 Call all hinders! If you feel there is any possibility
hitting your opponent, don't swing. Play the point ov

14 After the match, thank your opponent. Congratulate h
if he won.

WARMING UP

Before starting a game of racquetball, you should spend 5–10 minutes doing physical exercises designed to stretch and loosen your body's large muscle groups. Warming up, increasing metabolism, stretching tight muscles and ligaments, preparing your joints for movement, relaxing, increasing heart and lung action, and improving body coordination and motor patterns are all important when warming up. For racquetball, your leg, back, and upper body muscle groups should be given specific attention. It is very important that you *gradually* accustom yourself to intensive physical exercise. You should stretch slowly, without bobbing or jerking motions which may cause torn muscles.

EQUIPMENT

The racquet

Racquets are made from wood, fiberglass, and various metals, including aluminum. The racquet head may be one of two basic types—either teardrop, or rectangular-faced.

Weight   The weight of the racquet should be based on individual preference; however, most players prefer a light model that can be controlled easily. A racquet of improper weight can impede proper stroke development, so it should be selected with care. The following suggestions may be helpful:

light weight: 8–9 ounces (girls and women)
medium weight: 9–9½ ounces (boys and most men)
heavy weight: 9½–10 ounces (some men)

Teardrop (above) and rectangular (below) racquet designs

Metal vs. fiberglass   Fiberglass racquets, in general
are more flexible than metal ones. Their light weight and
flexibility make them popular with tournament players
who like longer contact between ball and racquet strings
for better control.

Since aluminum racquets are stiffer than fiberglass, the
ball comes off the racquet faster. So, if you want to play
a hard-driving, power game, aluminum should be your
choice. They are good all-around racquets, due to their
light weight, durability, and added power.

There is quite a difference in how the various racquets
perform, especially when it comes to flexibility, or stiff-
ness. Before you buy a racquet, try several brands. Pick
them up and swing them a few times, testing their weight
and handling ease. Remember that racquet choice is mostly
a matter of personal preference. Make sure it feels good to
you before buying it.

Try a few racquets before making
your choice

Type	Advantages	Disadvantages
wood	inexpensive ($5–$10)	very heavy, bulky
fiberglass	light weight, best control, medium priced ($10—$35)	not as durable as metal
aluminum	most durable, light weight, greater power than fiber-glass	most expensive ($20–$50)

Strings   Most racquets are strung with nylon; however
gut and monofilament strings are available. Nylon is relatively cheap ($5–$10), and usually lasts a long time. Gut
is the most expensive ($10–$30), does not wear as long
as nylon, but has a little more resilience. It has little advantage over nylon in racquetball.

In regard to string tension, players vary in their prefer-
ences. Generally, fiberglass racquets should be strung between 23 and 28 pounds tension, aluminum and metal
racquets between 28 and 35 pounds. As the tension in-
creases the ball comes off the strings faster, requiring better
ball and racquet control for accurate shots.

Handle grips   Grips are usually composed of rubber
or leather. Leather grips wear down faster than rubber, but
they provide a more secure handhold. Both rubber and
leather grips can be washed with soap and water.

The circumference of the racquet handle determines the
size of the grip. Since the wrist is used extensively in rac

quetball, grip sizes are usually smaller than tennis grips. If you play tennis, make sure the grip is smaller than the one on your tennis racquet. A grip that is too large can greatly reduce your hitting power. A small grip can be enlarged, but usually a large grip cannot be reduced. As a general rule in selecting the proper grip size, your two middle fingers should just touch your palm as you wrap your fingers around the handle. Grip sizes usually range between 3¹⁵⁄₁₆ inches and 4⅜ inches.

Care   Metal and fiberglass racquets require virtually no care. If your racquet does not have a strip of plastic on the rim of the frame, one can be purchased. This piece acts as a cushion, and protects both racquet and wall during shots in close quarters.

Eye guards

Eye guards or prescription athletic glasses are highly recommended for racquetball play. Serious eye damage, even loss of sight, can be caused by balls traveling at speeds up to 100 m.p.h., or even by the edge of a racquet. Many professionals wear eye guards in competition as well as in practice, and advise their use. Possessing more ball control and experience, advanced players run a much smaller risk of getting injured. Beginning players, however, should wear eye protection at all times.

A high speed ball, and eye protection

The ball

There are a number of good brands of balls manufactured today, and they cost approximately $1–$2 each.

Gloves

Gloves are worn by many players to help prevent the racquet from slipping in their hands. They can be cleaned with soap and water. Most gloves are made of leather, so don't dry them over heat, or they will dry up and become hard. As they begin to dry, put them on your hand to stretch and soften them. Two pairs of gloves used alternately between washings will each last longer than a single pair used constantly.

Dress

The only dress requirement for racquetball is that your clothes fit comfortably. Shorts and a light shirt, or t-shirt, are recommended. Women sometimes wear tennis dresses. All players should use rubber-soled shoes, and socks. For tournaments, your clothing must be light in color, since dark shades can camouflage the ball. Head and wrist bands will help keep perspiration from your eyes and hands.

GRIPPING THE RACQUET

Of all the fundamentals in racquetball, nothing is more basic than the way you grip the racquet. Your grip determines how and where you hit the ball as it makes contact with the strings.

In racquetball there are three basic grips: The most popular are the Eastern and the Continental, which are used for both forehand and backhand shots. The Western grip is used only in special instances. It is best to experiment in order to find out which grip you prefer.

The racquet handle has eight edges, or "bevels," all with specific names. Examine the diagram and learn them before you continue.

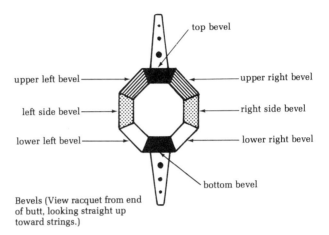

Bevels (View racquet from end of butt, looking straight up toward strings.)

All grip and stroke instructions are written for right-handed players, so if you're left handed you'll have to do a bit of reversing.

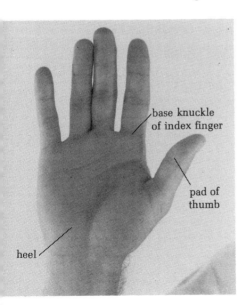

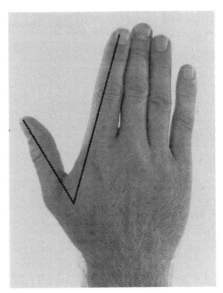

Check the position of these key points on your hand as you experiment with basic racquet grips. Left: key palmar points. Right: "V" crease between thumb and forefinger

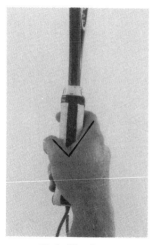

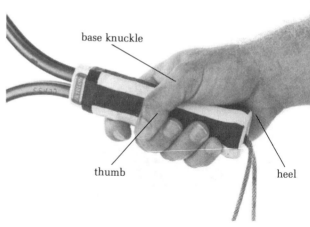

base knuckle

thumb

heel

Heel of hand on
the upper right bevel

Pad of thumb on
the left side bevel

Base knuckle on
the right side bevel

"V" in the middle
or slightly left
of middle
top bevel

Eastern forehand grip

Place the heel of your right hand on the racquet grip's uppe
right bevel with the pad of your thumb on the left side
bevel. When you close your fingers around the racquet
the base knuckle of your index finger should rest on the
right side bevel. The "V" formed with your thumb and
index finger should run down the middle of the top beve
(or slightly to the left of the middle).

Another way to approach this grip is to hold the racquet
in your left hand so that its edges are perpendicular to the
ground, then place your right hand on the strings and run
the hand down the throat until you reach the grip. Now
wrap your fingers around the grip so that your thumb
touches your middle finger, and your index finger ex
tends up the grip.

The Eastern forehand is often referred to as the "shake
hands" grip. It is used to hit forehand shots.

Eastern forehand grip—alternate
approach

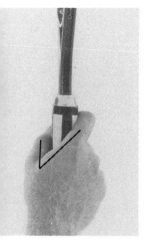

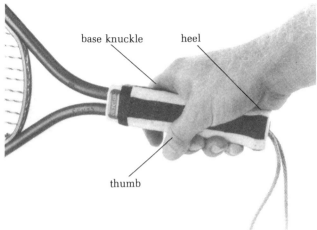

base knuckle   heel

thumb

Heel of hand on top bevel

Pad of thumb diagonally
across the lower left
and left side bevels

Base knuckle on the top
or slightly to the right
of the top bevel

"V" in the middle
of the left side bevel

Eastern backhand grip

If you decide to use the Eastern forehand grip, then you
must use the Eastern backhand with it, in order to hit a
good backhand shot.

To switch to the Eastern backhand grip, rotate your hand
one quarter turn to the left (counterclockwise) from the
Eastern forehand. The heel of your hand should now be
on the top bevel, and the pad of your thumb should run
diagonally across the lower left or left side bevels, which-
ever feels more comfortable. The base knuckle of the index
finger should rest on the top bevel, or just to the right of
the top bevel. The "V" between your thumb and index
finger should run down the middle of the left side bevel.

The backhand grip may feel a little uncomfortable to beginners. Combined with the proper stroke, however, it will
give you maximum power and efficiency on your backhand shots.

Common faults

1 *The fingers are too close together in a "fist"
grip.*
2 *The hand is too far down, on the end of the
racquet. Choke up.*

Switching grips with the Eastern

You must switch your grip from forehand to backhand
whenever you want to hit a backhand shot. If you don't,
the racquet face will be tilted backwards when ball contact is made. Your shot will lose its speed, and angle too
high on the wall.

Initially, before hitting the ball, you should grasp the racquet with the Eastern forehand grip. Hold the throat of your racquet lightly with your left hand. If you see the ball coming to your backhand (left) side, guide the racquet back with your left hand. Your grip should begin to change as you start this motion. The actual switch can be accomplished by either turning the racquet clockwise with your left hand, or by moving your right hand counterclockwise around the handle. The change should be completed well before your backswing has been completed. Like the majority of racquetball fundamentals, grip adjustment will become a habit with practice.

Continental grip

Unlike the Eastern style, which differentiates between the forehand and backhand grips, the Continental forehand and backhand are the same. The advantage of the Continental is that during fast play no time is required to change grips. If you choose this style you must make sure that your arm is in the proper position: Rotate it forward slightly or you will lose control and power.

Heel of hand on part of the top and upper right bevels

Pad of thumb diagonally across the left side bevel

Base knuckle on the upper right bevel

"V" in the middle of the upper left bevel

For the Continental grip, rotate your hand one eighth of a turn to the left (counterclockwise) from the Eastern forehand grip. The heel of your hand should rest on part of the top bevel and on the upper right bevel, and the pad of your thumb should run diagonally across the left side bevel. The base knuckle of your index finger should be on the upper right bevel. If you are gripping correctly, the "V" between your index finger and thumb will run down the middle of the upper left bevel.

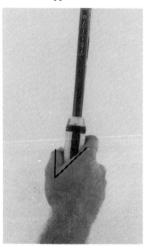

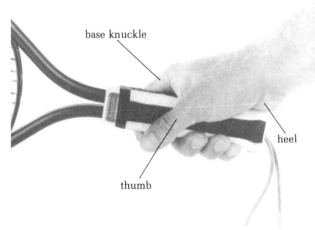

base knuckle

heel

thumb

Continental grip

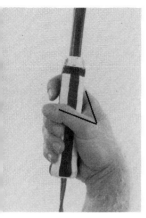

Heel of hand on the lower right and bottom bevels

Pad of thumb on top bevel

Base knuckle on the lower right bevel

"V" runs down the edge of the upper right and right side bevels

Western grip

The Western grip should be used to hit the forehand ceiling shot only. Actually, any of the forehand grips can be used for ceiling shots, but the advantage of the Western is that it opens the racquet face, making the shot an easier one.

To achieve the Western grip from the Eastern forehand, rotate your hand a full one quarter turn to the right (clockwise). The heel of your hand will be on the lower right and bottom bevels, while the pad of your thumb will rest on the top bevel. The base knuckle of your index finger should be on the lower right bevel, and your thumb and index finger "V" should run down the edge of the upper right and right side bevels.

Another way to get the feeling of this grip is to lay the racquet down on the ground, then pick it up. Your hand will automatically be in the Western grip position.

FUNDAMENTAL STROKES

The basic racquetball strokes are similar to those used in tennis, with one important exception: In racquetball your wrist is used extensively. Whether you've played tennis or not, you'll find that you can master the strokes with just a little practice. Pay attention to the following five maneuvers when performing any stroke. Several maneuvers have been broken down into parts, for easier explanation. Remember that even though we speak of separate parts of a swing, the stroke must be one smooth, continuous motion.

1 Ready Position
    Stance
    Grip
2 Backswing
    Pivot
    Body angle
    Moving to the ball
    Weight distribution
    Racquet position
3 Forward Swing
    Racquet and body position
    Weight transfer and rotation
    Point of contact
4 Follow-through
5 Recovery to Ready Position

Since the principles for forehand and backhand shots are almost identical, the following discussion applies to both of them, except when specifically noted.

1. Ready position

Prior to each forehand or backhand shot, you must assume the ready position. Place your feet about shoulder-width apart (1), with your knees slightly flexed (2) and your weight balanced equally on the balls of each foot (3). Your back should be bent slightly (4), and your head up (5). Your racquet is held in front of you (6), with a comfortable bend at your elbows. Hold the racquet in your forehand grip.

From this position you can move in any direction, and hit any stroke. After every shot, attempt to set up your ready position at mid court, just behind the short line.

Common faults

1 *The player stands "flatfooted."*
2 *The knees are too straight and stiff.*
3 *The racquet is held below waist level, down near the knees.*

ady position

2. Backswing

The essence of a good forehand or backhand is in early preparation, which begins with the backswing. An early backswing allows you to react to unusual bounces, to stroke the ball properly, and to hit a greater number of offensive shots. This maneuver should begin as soon as you can tell whether the ball is coming to your forehand or backhand, preferably before it strikes the floor. As soon as you can determine the ball's direction, you should ad-

just your grip, if necessary, and pivot your body (whi(
will aid your backswing):

Forehand pivot   The hips (7) and shoulders (8) turn ?
degrees, so that they are facing the right side wall. T**
feet merely twist in place (9).

Backswing (forehand pivot)

Backhand pivot   The procedure is reversed: You tu*
your hips and shoulders toward the left side wall. T*
body turn is a little greater on the backhand; you shou*
almost be looking at the front wall over your front should*

Body angle   After the hips and shoulders have p*
oted, take a step forward with your front foot (10) (l*
foot for forehand, right for backhand). Your entire bo*
should now be parallel with the side wall (11).

Backswing (backhand pivot)

Moving to the ball   Once you have pivoted, you m*
move to the exact location on the court where you c*
meet the ball squarely. The success of this action depen*
upon quick and accurate judgment, which can only *
gained by experience.

et position (forehand)

Set position   After moving to the ball, you should make sure that you are in the proper set position. Make sure your knees are comfortably bent, and your feet are not too far apart. You should be facing the side wall. In the set position the racquet can be in one of two places: (a) straight back, pointing at the back wall, or, more commonly, (b) pointed at the ceiling with the arm bent approximately 90 degrees (12). The upper arm (13) should be parallel to the floor, with the wrist bent backward (14) in a cocked position.

Weight distribution   Initially, while pivoting, your weight should be on the front foot. When you are getting into the set position, your weight is on the rear foot (15).

et position (backhand)

> **Common faults**
> 1 The backswing is not started soon enough.
> 2 The player does not pivot his body and hips sideways.
> 3 The backswing is too low, causing loss of racquet speed and power.
> 4 The wrist is not cocked, and is too stiff.
> 5 The weight is not on the back foot.
> 6 The stance is too wide. The feet should be shoulder width apart.
> 7 The elbow is too close to the body. The arm should not be touching the player's side, and it should be bent comfortably.

3. Forward swing

Weight transfer and rotation　The forward swing should start with the weight shifting (16) from your back foot to your front foot. As you transfer your weight, your shoulders and hips (17) should begin to rotate toward the front wall. This rotation is easier if you bend your back leg inward (18), and slightly toward the floor.

Hint

During the swing, lift the heel of your back foot off the ground, so that your toe scrapes the floor. This will automatically turn your hips and shoulders for you.

Point of contact　For the forehand stroke, your elbow should lead (19) as you begin the downward arc of your swing. The ball should come in contact with your racquet at a point opposite the instep of your front foot (20). For the backhand stroke, the point of contact should be about 6 inches in front of your instep, or just before the ball reaches your front foot. For a powerful shot on both the forehand and backhand, the wrist is snapped forward (21) as ball contact is made. This snap should be firm, not flimsy, facilitating an accurate shot.

Forward swing (forehand)

The ball is usually hit at one of three basic points: out of the air, immediately after it bounces and begins its upward arc, or after the bounce and near the end of its downward arc. The best spot to strike the ball is at ankle level, after it has bounced, at the end of its downward arc. Not only will this give you more time to get into position, you will also have a better chance of making a kill shot. You should, however, practice hitting balls coming at you at different heights.

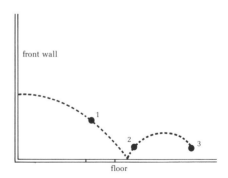

Three places to contact the ball:
(1) Volley or Fly; (2) Half-volley;
(3) Ideal place for good control

Common faults

1 The player swings only with the arms,
rather than making an entire body motion.
2 The player's forward swing is cramped,
thereby striking the ball too close to the body.
3 The head lifts, causing the player to lose
sight of the ball.
4 The ball is hit too far behind the front foot.
5 The knees are too stiff upon ball contact.
6 The racquet is not parallel to the ground
upon ball contact.
7 The player hits both the forehand and the
backhand with the same side of the racquet.
8 The elbow is snapped, causing a slap or
poke at the ball, instead of a firm stroke.

There are two separate opinions concerning the best position of the racquet face during ball contact:

The face can be either flat (perpendicular to the ground) or open (tilted back slightly). The advantage of the open-faced position is that it will give the ball underspin, causing it to bounce lower than a flat-stroked ball. The drawback of this method is that it may cause the ball to "float," and hit too high off the front wall. Those who favor the flat racquet face maintain that too much power and control are lost when the racquet is tilted.

Beginning players should try both of these styles. Decide on one and practice it! Ball control and speed are developed with experience.

4. Follow-through

The follow-through should be practiced along with all the other parts of the swing. It will add power to your stroke, and put you in better position to recover for the next shot. Let your racquet arm swing naturally across your body after ball contact is made.

At the completion of the follow-through, you should check your body for several key positions: The body should be bent low to the ground (22), the eyes (23) still focused on the ball. The front knee should be slightly bent (24), and the back knee should be bent at almost a 90-degree angle (25). The front foot should be flat on the floor (26), and the shoulders and hips (27) should be rotated facing the front wall. To help this rotation, the back heel should be lifted (28), with the toes scraping the floor. The racquet arm should be only slightly bent (29), and the racquet hand should end up in front of the opposite shoulder (30).

Follow-through (forehand)

ollow-through (backhand)

Common faults
1 *Body is too stiff and rigid. The legs are not bent.*
2 *The player does not follow through far enough.*

5. Recovery
Return quickly to the ready position by swinging your right foot around to a position parallel with your left. You are now prepared to hit a ball coming to either side of your body.

Forehand ceiling stroke

Forehand ceiling stroke

The basic maneuvers for this stroke are similar to those for the regular forehand, with a few important differences:

a) When possible, the racquet should be held in the Western grip, but any of the forehand grips may be used.

b) Instead of pivoting sideways, the shot can be made facing the front wall. Better balance and power are achieved, however, if you use the regular forehand pivot.

c) On the backswing, the racquet should be brought back to a position behind your head. The bend at your elbow should be approximately 90 degrees. This motion is a circular one.

d) In the set position, the racquet is directly behind your back, with your elbow pointed toward the ceiling. The higher you raise your elbow, the lower the racquet will drop, allowing more arc and power in your swing.

e) The forward swing should be directed upward, with the elbow leading. Your entire body, including your arm, should be fully extended toward the ceiling. The wrist snap is made upward just before ball contact.

f) The ball is met about a foot in front of the body, with the racquet tilted back, which will give a slight underspin to the ball. The higher ball contact is made, the better your chances are of its being a powerful shot.

g) To exaggerate your follow-through, let your right arm touch your left hip. Trying to stop your stroke too early may result in damaged forearm muscles, or "racquetball elbow."

h) Beginners should facilitate recovery by keeping their balance, and anchoring their feet. Advanced players will often take a step forward during their follow-through, ending the stroke with their feet crossed.

Common faults

1 *The weight does not shift to the front foot upon ball contact.*

2 *The racquet stops behind the head, losing momentum during the backswing.*

3 *The ball is allowed to drop too low so that it is impossible to hit it with the arm fully extended. This results in a "pushing" stroke, instead of a circular one.*

Backhand ceiling stroke

Backhand ceiling stroke

This stroke is perhaps one of the hardest to perfect. T form for the backhand ceiling stroke is similar to the re ular backhand stroke, except that the ball is contacte near shoulder level, approximately arm's length away fro the body. Because this stroke has to be hit with power, sure that all your weight is transferred to your front fo during the upward swing. Upper body rotation is al important.

Overhead stroke

The overhead stroke is performed in exactly the sam manner as the ceiling shot, with two exceptions:

a) The regular forehand grip is used.

b) The wrist snap at the point of contact is a forwa motion. By snapping your wrist over the top of t ball, the overhead can be hit with considerable spee

This stroke is used primarily in the backcourt when t ball is above shoulder height. The decision to use eith the ceiling stroke or the overhead stroke depends on t type of return you want to make. While the ceiling stro is used only for the ceiling shot, the overhead stroke c be used to hit driving pass shots, lobs, backcourt kills (n advised), and even ceiling shots, when you are unable change your grip quickly enough.

Overhead stroke

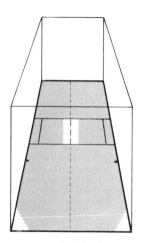

Most serves should be hit from the center of the service zone

The corners are the best spots to place your serves. Direct most of them to the opponent's backhand side

SERVES

One of the most important shots, if not the most important is the serve. It is the only time in the match when you are in complete control. Without it, you cannot score points with it, you cannot lose any points. Think offensively. A well-hit serve may not win the point immediately, but it will often result in a weak return, giving you an easy put-away.

Basically, there are four types of serves: the drive, the cross-court (including the Z), the lob, and the garbage serves. Each service, along with its variations, should eventually be learned. Initially, a player must also acquaint himself with some general guidelines that apply to all serves:

a) When you get into the service box, relax for a few seconds before serving. Don't rush. Take a deep breath, and gather all your energy. You are in control.

b) Stand in the center of the service zone. (For certain serves you will be located one or two feet to either side.) By standing too close to either side wall, you will be surrendering the important center court position and limiting your choice of service direction. In addition, by assuming a central position you will have a better chance of disguising serves directed toward the forehand or backhand corners.

c) Before serving, form a mental picture, detailing what the serve will look like. Then determine where you must place the shot on the front wall for accurate results.

d) Although the serve is hit with the basic forehand or backhand, you should use your best stroke, usually the forehand. If you develop the same swing style for your various serves, your opponent will not be able to tell which one is coming.

e) By taking advantage of your opponent's weaknesses, you can make your serve an offensive weapon. Analyze his game, and direct your serve toward his poorest shot. The more difficulty you cause him the weaker his returns will be, perhaps giving you a chance to make a kill shot, or a put-away. Determine on which side you will serve the ball, how fast you'll serve it, and how high. In playing an opponent for the first time, serve to his backhand first.

f) Once you have mastered all the serves, mix them up; don't be predictable. If, however, you cannot hit all serves with equal skill, stay with your best one. Don't hit a weak serve just to change serves.

For the service, you must bounce the ball before hitting it. The ball must first hit the front wall, then cross the short line on the fly, in order to be considered "good." If

it does not pass the short line, it is a fault. The ball may hit either of the side walls, but not both. *If you hit three walls, including the front wall, it is a fault.* A serve that hits the ceiling or back wall after hitting the front wall is also a fault. If you hit two consecutive faults, you lose your serve. Any serve that hits a wall other than the front wall first, is an out.

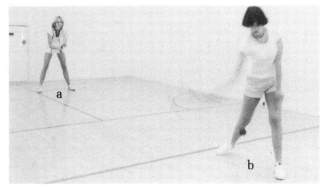

Receiving (a) and serving (b) positions

Drive serve

This is the serve which is used most frequently. It is hit hard and low off the front wall, and forces the receiver to react very quickly. If hit accurately, the drive is very effective in keeping your opponent off balance, guessing where the ball will rebound.

Use the basic forehand stroke. Ball contact should be made at a height between your ankle and knee. Since maximum power is needed, make sure your weight has shifted to your front foot, and that you get good upper body rotation. Try to hit the front wall at a slight angle, 1–3 feet above the floor. This height will vary greatly, depending on how much power is exerted during the serve.

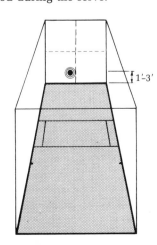

1'-3'

rive serve

Target area for a drive serve directed at a right-handed opponent's backhand

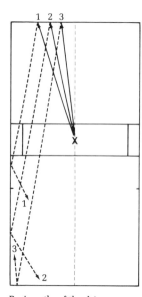

Basic paths of the drive serve

With practice, your drive serve will rebound off the fro
wall and bounce:

1) Just behind the short line, and low on the side wa
   near the crotch.
2) Deep off the side wall, near the back wall.
3) To the backhand or forehand rear corners, withou
   hitting the side wall.

As with any other stroke, the execution of the drive ser
must be exact or you will set your opponent up for an ea
return.

Common faults

1 The server contacts the ball too high. The
ball should be hit at knee level, preferably
lower.

2 The player sacrifices control for speed. Hit
the ball only as hard as accuracy will allow.

3 The ball strikes too hard, and high, off the
front wall, and rebounds sharply off the
back wall for an easy set-up. The ball must
not rebound off the back or side walls too
far into center court.

4 The angle of service is too sharp, causing
the ball to rebound off the side wall into
center court for an easy set-up. To be effective, the serve should rebound to a point
no more than three feet from the back wall.

5 The server hits too many drive serves to
the opponent's forehand. About one out of
five serves—just enough to keep your opponent from anticipating its direction—
should be hit to the forehand corner.

Variations   The three-quarter drive, or off-speed driv
serve is hit with a motion identical to that used for the lo
drive serve. The ball, however, travels at a speed one-ha
to three-quarters as fast as the regular drive. Vary the heig
of this serve by striking the ball at waist level. The ba
will rebound higher, making it difficult for the oppone
to hit a kill return.

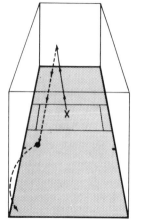

Path of the three-quarter drive

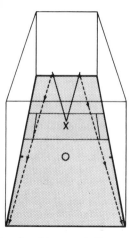

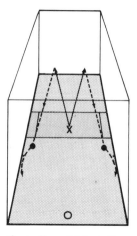

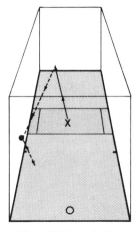

ep, low drive serve to the corners. Effective when the opponent is slow, or playing too ●se

Short, off speed drive to the forehand or backhand

Low side-wall drive to the backhand. Effective when the opponent is playing too deep

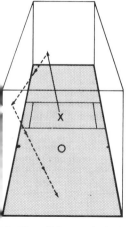

gh side-wall drive to the backnd. Effective when the opponent is playing too close

Pointers   a) If your opponent is slow or tired, the drive should be served deep to both corners. b) If your opponent is playing too far back, a short drive serve that lands just behind the short line, or behind the short line near the crotch, is effective. The ball will probably bounce twice, before he can react. However, if not hit perfectly, these serves will give your opponent an easy shot. c) If your opponent is playing too far forward, a deep drive, or a drive that hits about three feet high on the side wall, is effective. The deep drive will go past him quickly, making it very difficult to get to the ball; the high side wall drive will bounce behind him for a possible winner. However, if you fail to carom the ball behind your opponent, he will surely have an easy set-up, and will "kill" the ball.

ective drive serve keeps receiver off balance

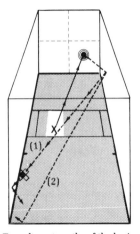

Two alternate paths of the basic cross-court serve to the backhand. Both serves must bounce on the floor before hitting the third wall

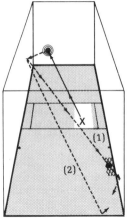

Two alternate paths of the basic cross-court serve

Cross-court serve

Once the drive serve is mastered, the cross-court can ▮ learned easily. Using your forehand stroke, hit the ball ▮ it strikes the front wall approximately 3–4 feet from th▮ right corner, and about three feet above the floor. It wi▮ rebound sharply onto the side wall, and bounce deep in▮ the left rear corner. All cross-court serves bound into th▮ backhand corner (if your opponent is right handed).

In order to get a better angle for this serve, stand one ▮ two feet to the left of the service zone's center point. Yc▮ should serve carefully, since the ball must strike the fro▮ wall before it strikes the side wall, or else it will be call▮ an "out."

Reverse cross-court   Use the same technique as f▮ the regular cross-court serve, but stand one or two feet ▮ the right of the center point, and direct your shot towa▮ the left front corner. It will rebound into the right re▮ corner, or to your opponent's forehand.

Variations   The cross-court serve can be hit so that ▮ either rebounds off the side wall or travels directly fro▮ the front wall to the back wall. The closer the ball is ▮ to the front wall corner, the greater the chance that it w▮ carom off the side wall. You should practice hitting ba▮ at various spots on the front wall to perfect your cros▮ court serves.

Pointers   Used in conjunction with the drive serve, t▮ cross-court serve becomes a very effective weapon. Aft▮ hitting several drive serves to one rear corner, you can p▮ your opponent seriously off balance if you hit a cros▮ court serve to the opposite corner. His return is likely ▮ be very weak. Another advantage is that the ball dies clo▮ to the back wall, or rebounds at unusual angles, if th▮ serve is executed properly.

Z serve

The Z serve is very similar to the basic cross-court serv▮ It derives its name from the "Z" pattern which the b▮ makes during its flight from the right front to the left re▮ corner of the court. When hit to the right rear corner, t▮ path follows a "backward Z" pattern, resulting in a rever▮ Z serve. Both of these serves can be divided into the l▮ hard Z and the high Z variations:

Low hard Z   The low Z serve is extremely diffic▮ to execute; if hit improperly, it will surely lose the ral▮ It is extremely effective, however, when performed a▮ curately.

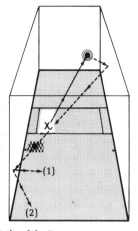

aths of the Z serve
) Ball will rebound off the
side wall almost parallel to
the backwall if hit very hard
with a live ball
) Path of Z serve when hit with
moderate speed off the front
wall

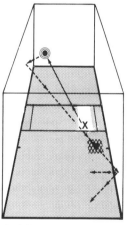

ath of the reverse Z serve

The correct serving position is to the left of the service box's center point. The closer you stand to the left side wall, the easier it becomes to hit the Z serve. But you must try not to move so far out of the center position that your opponent will guess your serve, or so far in that you will be out of position for the return.

The low hard Z serve is carried out with the same motion as the drive serve. The ball should contact the right front wall about three feet off the floor, and 1–2 feet to the left of the side wall. After hitting the front wall, the ball ricochets into the right side wall, and then travels across court toward the left rear corner. After bouncing on the floor, the ball hits the left side wall, and rebounds sharply off of it.

If hit with enough force, this serve puts a tremendous amount of spin on the ball, causing it to rebound off the left side wall *parallel* to the back wall. This type of rebound will confuse all but the highly skilled player. The closer the ball contacts the front corner upon service, the greater its chances of rebounding in this parallel fashion. If you do not hit the low Z correctly, the ball will head diagonally toward the back wall. It will carry too deep and rebound off the back wall, or come off the left side wall too early, for an easy set-up.

High Z The high Z serve is essentially a high cross-court serve, not a typical Z serve. It is a change-of-pace serve, not hit with as much power as the low Z and drive serves. Again, it should be initiated from a position in the service box just to the left of center. The ball is struck with an upward motion to "lift" it close to the ceiling. It should contact the front wall about 15 feet above the floor, close to the right side wall. It will then ricochet into

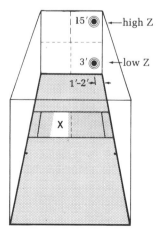

Z serve target areas, and position
in service box

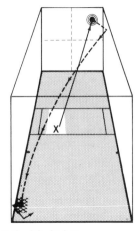

Path of the high Z serve

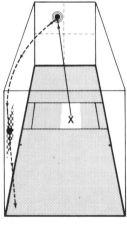

The lob serve should be aimed 1-2 feet off center and must brush the side wall on the downward trajectory

the right side wall, travel in a high arc toward the left rear corner, strike the floor, hit the left side wall with diminished speed, and finally drop in the corner near the back wall.

The high Z serve must not hit the ceiling (a fault). To be effective, it should hit the side wall deep in the rear corner after hitting the floor.

High Z pointers   The advantage of the high Z is that must be hit by your opponent before it bounces, or it will almost surely die as it strikes the back wall. In order to make a good return, your opponent must be extremely alert. Because the ball is moving off speed, the receiver must meet the ball squarely and accurately, or his return will be weak. The Z serve forces your opponent to hit high ball out of the air, or dig the shot out of the corner which often results in an easy set-up for the server.

Lob serve

The lob serve is used mainly at beginning and intermediate levels of play. It is an off-speed shot, which rebounds high off the front wall. Ideally, the ball will slightly graze the side wall, slow down, and die as it reaches the back wall.

This serve is accomplished by hitting the ball on an upward arc so it strikes the front wall, about three-quarters of the way up, close to the side wall. The racquet face tilted backward a bit, allowing the ball to travel in an upward direction. The lob may be hit from the center of the service box, but the best results are obtained by standing to the right or left of this spot while aiming the serve in cross-court direction.

Pointers   The lob is a good change-of-pace serve when used against an opponent who likes to hit the ball hard consistently. You should be extremely careful when using

Lob serve

it: If the ball does not hit the side wall, your opponent will be able to hit the ball in mid-air. If he lets it strike the back wall, it will usually hit too hard, giving him an easy shot. To help reduce the chances of a kill return, the lob should be directed toward your opponent's backhand.

arget area for garbage serve

Garbage serve

This serve certainly looks like "trash"; you would swear that the player employing it does not know how to play the game. Yet many top professionals use the garbage serve, and consider it their most effective "bread-and-butter" serve. Since it is a change-of-pace serve, it must be executed with a soft touch. The actual serving motion is similar to the lob's.

ote difference between point of contact for garbage serve (left) and point of contact for drive serve (right)

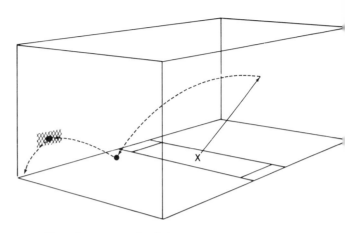

The garbage serve can brush the
side wall . . .

The ball must be struck at a point between the waist ar
chest, and should be aimed just to the left of the front wal
center point. After rebounding, it should bounce ne
mid court, and brush the side wall near the back wall. A
alternative method is to have the ball travel directly
the back wall, where it should rebound into an imagina
two-foot square in the corner. If it rebounds further th
this, your opponent will have an easy shot.

Pointers   If executed correctly, the garbage serve w
end up in the rear corner, at chest height. Your oppone

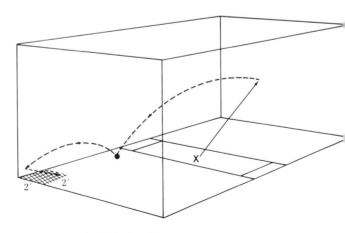

Or it may hit the back wall
directly if it rebounds into a
two-foot square

will be forced to hit a ceiling shot return. For these reasons, it can be valuable if you are playing against someone who is killing many of your low drive serves. To an inexperienced player, the garbage serve appears ridiculously simple to kill or pass. On the contrary, it will usually cause either an error by your opponent, or an easy set-up for you.

As you practice, experiment. What happens when you hit a drive serve closer to the side wall? Does a slight position change in the service zone have an effect on the serve? Try hitting the ball at different speeds, and at different spots, on the front wall. Don't forget that all serves can be directed to both sides of the court. Practice each serve until the stroke becomes fluid and natural. To accomplish this, master each serve separately; be sure of one before continuing on to the next. Concentrate on developing a good basic serve, then use the others to complement it. Don't forget to attack your opponent's weakness—usually his backhand.

OFFENSIVE SHOTS

With practice, you will find yourself rapidly progressin
beyond the beginning level of play. At the intermedia
and advanced levels, a majority of the shots become offe
sive in nature. In other words, they are performed with t
intention of ending the rally outright, with a gain of a poi
or the serve. The skilled racquetball player is able to h
winning offensive shots in various situations.

Kill shot

This is the most effective offensive shot in racquetba
no advancing player can do without it. When it is hit cc

rectly, the kill offers little or no chance for a return. All the variations (except the overhead kill) are executed with the basic forehand and backhand strokes. A general rule to keep in mind is that the ball should hit the front wall very close to the bottom, allowing it to rebound only a few inches above the floor.

Path of a good kill shot

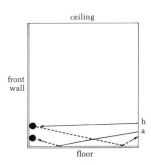

Path of a poor kill shot:
a. Ball hits floor first
b. Ball hits front wall too high

Common faults

1 The ball is hit too low so it hits the floor before reaching the front wall, resulting in a sideout or point for the opponent.

2 The ball is hit too high off the front wall so it rebounds into the court where an opponent can easily reach the ball.

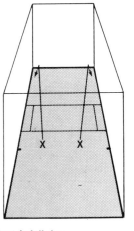

straight kill shot

Straight kill   This power stroke, which accounts for approximately 70% of all kill shots, can be used anywhere on the court as long as there is enough room for a full swing, and your opponent is not directly in front of you. The shot can be tried from anywhere but is most successful from the front and middle court areas.

For both the forehand and backhand straight kills, the player should pivot toward the side wall and bend down as low as possible. This exaggerated flex at the hips and knees is necessary in order to accomplish a swing which allows the racquet to travel parallel to the ground and contact the ball at calf level, or lower. Not only does this motion assure low ball placement, but it also helps the player to snap his wrist more easily, for more power. A swing that is parallel to the floor will prevent the player

from driving the ball down into the floor, or excessivel
high against the front wall. Ball contact should be mad
at a point even with the heel of your front foot. The fore
hand straight kill should be directed to the forehand corne
of the front wall, and the backhand kill to the backhan
corner.

Pinch kill (side wall–front wall)   For this shot, whic
is the hardest of all kills to retrieve, the ball is hit low an
with moderate force to either side wall and from there re
bounds into the front wall. Because the ball loses momen
tum on the rebound and tends to die upon reaching th
front wall, this shot does not have to be hit as low or a
hard as other kills. Occasionally, an "off-speed" or "soft
pinch makes for an effective change of pace. Although th
shot can be executed anywhere on the court, it gets bes
results when:

a) The player is close to the forehand or the backhan
side wall, and the opponent is near him.

b) The opponent is behind the player.

c) The opponent is not watching the player.

The ball can be struck with the racquet face perpendicula
to the floor or slightly open. The advantage of a slightl
open face is that the ball can be more easily directed towar
the side wall, where it will rebound parallel to the floor

The ball can hit the side wall anywhere near the front wall
but for best results it should hit at least 3 feet from th
front wall. This will cause it to angle off the front wal
toward the opposite side wall and away from the oppo
nent, rather than heading into center court toward the op
ponent. If this shot is not hit low enough, or if it is hit to
hard, the ball will pop up into center court for an eas
return by an opponent.

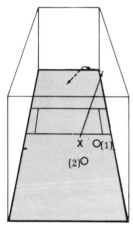

Pinch kill (1) (opponent near player)

Pinch kill (2) (opponent behind player)

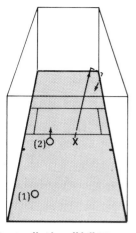

ront wall-side wall kill (1)
pponent in back court) (2)
pponent out of position,
nticipating pinch kill)

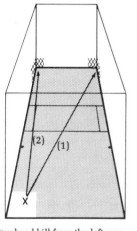

verhead kill from the left-rear
urt: Hit either cross-court (1) or
wn-the-line (2), to a 3 foot
quare area at either front wall
rner

Front wall–side wall kill   This kill shot should be attempted only if your opponent is in the back court, or he is out of position to make a good return. The ball is hit with the basic forehand or backhand stroke and strikes the front wall at either corner, no higher than thigh level. It will then angle into the closest side wall, and rebound onto the floor toward center court.

Since this shot has several drawbacks, it is the least often used of the kills: If the ball comes off the side wall angling wide, high, and toward center court, the opponent has an almost perfect setup. Should it hit the floor near the crotch of the front wall-side wall, it will tend to bounce high for another easy shot.

Overhead kill   The overhead kill differs from other kill shots in that the ball is contacted at shoulder height or above, rather than at waist level or below. Because it is nearly impossible to get a flat roll-out off the front wall with this shot, it is not considered a highly effective weapon by most players. The overhead kill is hit from the back court with a forehand motion similar to that used by a baseball pitcher. For a more comprehensive description of the stroke used, review the "forehand ceiling stroke" and "overhead stroke" sections on pages 25 and 26.

When this shot is properly executed, the ball strikes within a 3-foot square in either corner of the front wall, preferably having hit the near side wall first. Most overhead kills should be hit across court. This allows for a greater margin of error. The shot, in general, resembles a normal pinch shot, except it is more difficult to execute.

A long ceiling ball rally (which usually causes an opponent to lose concentration slightly) is the best time to use the overhead kill. It should never be attempted when your opponent is in the front court.

Pass shot
Since is does not require pinpoint accuracy, the pass is the easiest offensive shot to master. It is a power stroke, aimed to the side, where it will be out of reach of your opponent. Force must not be used to the detriment of accuracy, however, for a shot hit too high or too hard may come off the backwall for an easy set-up to the opponent. Use this shot at mid court, when you are not entirely positive that you can make an accurate kill. You may also employ it as a tactic to run down your opponent's energy, since he will be forced to chase the ball in order to retrieve it. It is important, however, not to give up an easy kill shot in favor of the less offensive pass, especially when you are in the front court. Another rule to remember is not to pass if you are deep in the backhand back court.

This shot can be made with the forehand, backhand, and overhead strokes. If ball contact is made near knee level,

Effective pass shots going past the opponent

the swing should be slightly upward. If it is made near waist level, the swing should be parallel to the floor. Also when you contact the ball at lower levels, you should use a more exaggerated bend at the waist and knees.

There are several court situations where a pass shot especially effective:

a) When an opponent is in front court, and you are behind.

b) When an opponent is out of position near a side wall.

c) When an opponent is edging or charging forward in anticipation of a kill shot.

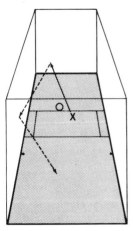

Cross-court pass (opponent in front court, player behind)

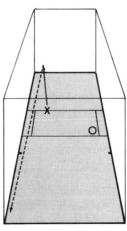

Down-the-wall pass (opponent on opposite side of court)

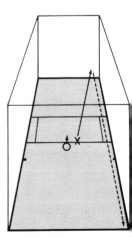

Down-the-wall pass (opponent near player and charging forward)

Down-the-line pass The body should be kept between the ball and the opponent when executing this variation of the pass. The ball should hit the front wall 1–3 feet from the side wall, 2–4 feet off floor level, and it should rebound parallel to the side wall. The shot is hit just hard enough so it does not rebound off the back wall. A common error is to cause the ball to hit the side wall after rebounding off the front wall, allowing it to bounce into center court for an opponent's easy retrieval. To correct this tendency, hit the ball farther away from the side wall, or with topspin or backspin. Backspin is preferred, as it will cause the ball to slide along the side wall rather than to pop out off the wall.

This pass shot is most effectively used on the backhand side. If it is directed toward the forehand, it must be performed perfectly in order to keep the ball out of your opponent's reach, since his forehand is probably his better stroke. Two good situations in which to use the down-the-line pass are:

    a) When standing in or near center court, with the opponent on the right or left.

    b) When standing on one side of the court, with the opponent on the opposite side.

Cross-court pass This shot is hit with about 80% of your full power, using either the basic forehand or backhand stroke. The ball is struck at a height between the knee and the waist, and should contact the front wall 2–4 feet off the floor. The ball travels in a "V" pattern from point of contact to termination. During the early learning stages of the game this shot is the easiest to develop. The fore-

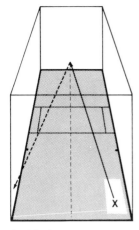

Path of the forehand cross-court pass

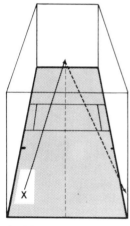

Path of the backhand cross-court pass

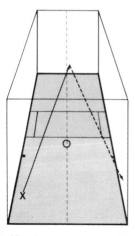

Backhand cross-court pass—Aim 1 foot off the center for an ideal shot

hand cross-court pass, in particular, can be termed the "bread and butter" shot of racquetball for four reasons:

a) When two right-handed or left-handed players are on the court, the forehand cross-court pass travels to the opponent's backhand.
b) The player hitting the shot is using his stronger stroke, the forehand.
c) The forehand cross-court shot is easily performed with a wide margin for error.
d) This shot can be used to return any ball coming toward the player's forehand, except for a well placed ceiling ball.

Generally, the player should aim his shot toward a spot on the front wall which is located about one foot to the right or left of the center point (depending on whether a backhand or forehand is being executed). This will ensure that the ball carries wide of the opponent's reach. It is better to err on the wide side rather than not to hit the shot wide enough.

Hints

1 Don't hit the ball so wide that it rebounds off the side wall in front of the opponent.
2 Don't hit the ball so hard that it will rebound far off the back wall.
3 To compensate for ball rise after racquet contact, the shot should be aimed at a point one foot below the 2–4 foot level on the front wall.
4 On a backhand cross-court pass, hit a wider-angled shot to make sure that it is farther away from the opponent's longer forehand reach.

The cross-court pass can be used to good advantage when:

a) Both opponent and player are standing on one side of the court, leaving the opposite side open.
b) Both opponent and player are in the front court or mid court, with the opponent in the center.
c) The opponent is "poaching," anticipating a kill shot.
d) The opponent is in center court and the player is presented with a setup in the three-quarter court area.

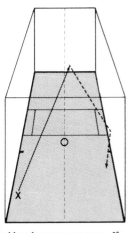

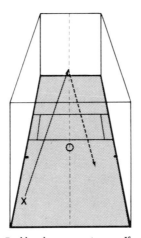

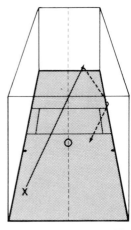

ckhand cross-court pass—If
e ball hits wider than 1 foot
f the center, at least there is a
od chance the rebound off the
de wall will "handcuff" the
ponent

Backhand cross-court pass—If
the ball is not hit wide enough
on the front wall, an easy shot is
left the opponent

Backhand cross-court pass—The
ball is hit too wide, and rebounds
off the side wall in front of the
opponent for an easy shot

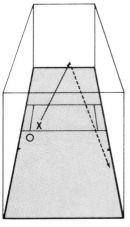

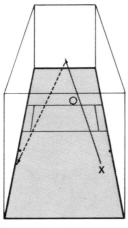

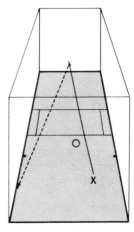

oss-court pass to the open side
the court

Cross-court pass when opponent
is anticipating a kill shot

Cross-court pass when opponent
is in center court and the player
has a "set-up"

Common faults (Pass shots)

1. *The player hits the ball too hard, or too high, causing it to rebound off the back wall.*

2 *The cross-court pass is not hit at a great enough angle.*

3 *Ball contact is made above the waist.*

Back wall shot

Back wall shot

Back wall play involves every situation where the ball contacts the back wall. If played properly, back wall shots can muster plenty of power since the player is moving along the same path as the ball: toward the front wall. It is possible to use almost any shot when returning the ball off the back wall, but the kill and pass are generally the best—either down the line, or across court. A helpful rule to follow is that you should use the same shots for balls coming off the back wall as you would for balls coming from the front.

Inexperienced players, in particular, are troubled by back wall play. They usually have a tendency to hit the ball in the air, using an overhead shot, rather than play the ball off the back wall. Another mistake is to chase the ball all the way to the back, rather than letting the ball rebound to them. These problems are slowly eliminated as the player improves his skill. A bit of good advice is to never hit a ball in the air if it can be played off the back wall.

The biggest problem in this type of play is getting into proper position to make a good shot. The secret of success lies in proper footwork. As the ball travels from the front wall to the back wall and rebounds, reversing direction, the player must be always moving along an identical path. When retreating to the back wall, a player must not back-pedal, or turn around and sprint. These two styles do not permit him to keep the ball in his sight throughout its path of travel.

The best retreat is the "sideways shuffle." To execute it you should turn 90 degrees, facing the side wall as you keep your eyes on the ball, and your racquet in the ready position. Then you should side pedal toward the back wall.

e "sideways shuffle" method
r retrieving shots off the back
all

There are two methods to play the ball off the back wa
the stop-and-step and the jog-and-hit. Usually the sto
and-step method is more effective on balls that do n
bounce off the back wall too far; the jog-and-hit is bett
on balls that rebound fairly hard.

Backwall rebounds

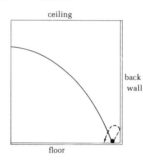 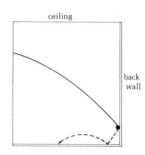

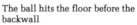

The ball hits the floor before the   The ball hits the floor after the
backwall   backwall

Stop-and-step   As the ball travels toward the ba
wall, the player trails it, moving in the same directio
When the ball strikes the back wall, the player stops a
plants himself in the same set position that is used f
a forehand or backhand stroke. Then the player steps in
the rebound as it travels forward and makes ball conta
in the proper position: off the heel of the lead foot on
forehand, and off the big toe on the backhand.

The crucial part of this method is where the player sto
and plants himself to await the rebounding ball. It is d
ficult to accurately estimate the correct setting-up distan
from the back wall. A most common error is to set up t
far from the rear wall, forcing ball contact to be made
behind the lead foot.

Jog-and-hit   The difference between this method a
the stop-and-step style is in the number of steps taken
a player when preparing to strike the ball. Normally on
one step is taken in the stop-and-step approach, compar
to three in the jog-and-hit. The advantage of this style
that more forward momentum is gathered, which is hel
ful for a more powerful stroke. Also, position adjustmer

Stop-and-step method

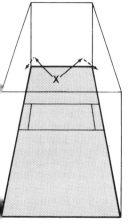

g-and-hit method

h of the drop shot executed
the front court

may be made while jogging, by lengthening or shortening the steps.

The jog-and-hit is initiated by retreating with the ball toward the back, and stopping and reversing direction as it bounces against the wall. When the player reverses direction, three forward steps are taken: lead foot first, followed by the rear foot behind the lead foot, and then the lead foot again. The player swings as the third step is made.

Common faults (Back wall shots)

1 *The player does not step into the ball on the hitting stroke. The body's weight is still on the back foot.*

2 *The player does not watch the ball at all times.*

3 *The player does not retreat far enough toward the back wall. Ball contact is made from behind the lead foot, causing the ball to travel into the side wall.*

Drop shot

The drop shot is considered offensive in nature since it ends the point if it is executed properly. It is most beneficially used as a surprise shot, or as a change of pace.

Although a drop shot may be employed anyplace on the court, including off the back wall, it is best to use it in the front court, when your opponent is near the back. Any of the basic strokes may be used for it, but the ball must be hit very softly, and low, against the front wall. The ball is usually directed to the wall's left or right corner. If it is hit with control, it will die after striking the front wall, and bounce twice before your opponent can reach it.

The drop shot requires great finesse. You must be deceptive to keep your opponent from anticipating it. Remember to use the same swing that you use for your basic forehand and backhand.

Strategy   If your opponent is slow, or tiring, a combination of lobs and drop shots will wear him out. If he is in the back third of the court, he will have to do that much more running to retrieve a drop.

The drop shot is especially effective against an opponent who turns his back to you when he is in the front center court position. It will usually catch him on his heels as he waits for the ball, expecting a more powerful shot.

DEFENSIVE SHOTS

In order to become a successful racquetball player, yo must learn to hit defensive shots which supplement yo offensive game. A good defensive shot will move yo opponent out of the important center court position, a will, in turn, allow you to move into better court positio Sound defensive knowledge and play will help preve your opponent from scoring.

The basic defensive shots are the ceiling, Z, around-th wall, lob, and overhead drive shots.

Ceiling shot

The ceiling shot has a particularly significant place racquetball. Besides being one of the shots most common used by tournament players, it has helped transform t game from a pure power contest to one in which patienc control, poise, and stamina are rewarded.

The ceiling shot is primarily a defensive one. It is us to keep the rally going, rather than to end it. It can, hov ever, become an offensive stroke, since it often forces yo opponent into making a weak return.

If the stroke is executed properly, the ball will first hit t ceiling 1–5 feet from the front wall; it will then rebou off the front wall, hit the floor, bounce deep into the ba court, come down along the back wall, and die. This rou makes the ball almost impossible to hit before it bounc in mid court. Consequently, your opponent must retu the ball from deep in the back court, above shoulder heig stifling his chances for a serious offensive shot.

Variation   The ceiling shot can also be used on t front court, by employing the "front-wall-first" method. is valuable when a hard hit ball comes to you at wa height while you are in a front court position. While kill shot would be difficult to execute in this situatic a front wall ceiling shot will allow you to remain in cent court, and at the same time force your opponent to the ba When correctly performed, the ball will first hit the fro wall about two feet below the ceiling, bound to the ceilir and then bounce deep into the back court. This variati should not be used while you are in the back court.

Strategy   A ceiling shot may be hit down the line, across court. The down-the-line ceiling shot, especia to the backhand, is usually the most effective. With pra tice, the ball can be made to "hug" the side wall on its w to the back wall. The advantage of this *wallpaper ball* that your opponent will have very little room for a fr swing, and a good return. Thus, a ceiling shot to the ba hand, which hugs the wall, can be an offensive maneuv

The wallpaper ball

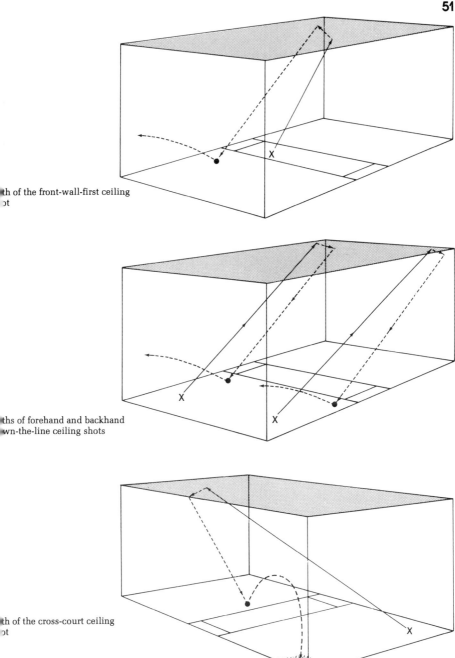

th of the front-wall-first ceiling
ot

ths of forehand and backhand
wn-the-line ceiling shots

th of the cross-court ceiling
ot

The cross-court ceiling shot is easier, and safer, to accomplish, but it is not as effective as the down-the-line. It is hit from a position right or left of center court, and aimed at the center of the ceiling. After striking the ceiling and front wall, the ball will take a path toward the corner which is opposite you.

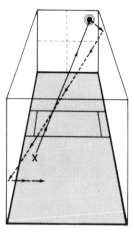

Path of the Z shot

Z shot

Even though the chances of making an error when usin this shot are high, it is nevertheless one of the most effe tive in the game. Since it is difficult to execute properl the Z shot is used sparingly, and only when the prop opportunity presents itself. It is primarily a defensi shot, effective in moving your opponent out of the cent court position, but it can be an offensive shot as well.

The Z shot is similar to the high Z serve. It can be us almost anywhere on the court; however the best positi is slightly off center, toward mid court. The ball should hit at an angle so it rebounds high off the front wall, ne the corner. It will then strike the side wall, travel diag nally across court without hitting the floor, and final rebound off the opposite side wall. The Z shot is uniq in that it rebounds off the final side wall parallel to t back wall. Normally, your opponent expects the ball bound off the side wall at an angle identical to the one which it hit the wall. Thus an inexperienced player will out of position to make a return. With practice, you will able to place the ball within a few feet of the back wa making a return by your opponent virtually impossib

This shot depends upon a good deal of power and accura for success. Since the Z carries a high risk of error, it mu be practiced thoroughly before using it in a game.

Around-the-wall shot

This shot resembles the Z ball in that it is hit high ar across court, but it hits the side wall first. From either si of the court, the ball is directed 12–15 feet up the opposi side wall and about 3 feet from the front wall. It shou

Hitting the around-the-wall shot

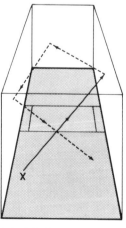

Path of the low around-the-wall shot

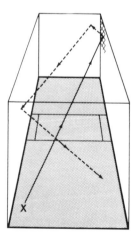

Path of the high around-the-wal shot, with the ball striking a three-foot square on the side wa

then rebound to the front wall, travel to the opposite side wall, and finally head on a diagonal toward the back corner.

The around-the-wall shot is primarily a defensive shot that forces your opponent to retreat out of center court position and into the back court. Care must be taken not to hit this shot too hard; otherwise, your opponent may have an easy retrieve off the back wall. The most effective around-the-wall shot begins to die before reaching the back wall. To defend against this shot, learn to intercept the ball in the air as it travels through center court toward the back corner.

Lob shot

Since 1971, when a livelier ball was introduced to racquetball, the lob shot has almost disappeared from advanced competition. For the most part, the ceiling shot has taken its place. But it is still a good maneuver for those players who lack the power to hit consistently good ceiling shots.

The lob shot is hit with very little power, with good control, and with the racquet face slightly open. The ball softly strikes the front wall near the top, and without touching the ceiling it bounces deep into the back court. If executed properly, the lob will just touch the side wall, slowing the ball so it dies as it reaches the back wall. If hit softly enough, the lob will float over your opponent's head, and force him out of center court.

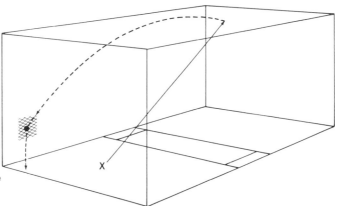

The lob shot must brush the side wall to be effective

Overhead drive shot

In execution, this shot is not as risky as the offensive overhead kill, so it should be used more frequently. Its primary purpose is defensive in nature—to keep an opponent in the back court. During a ceiling ball rally, when your opponent is moving to center court after each of his ceiling shots, the overhead drive is very effective. In this case,

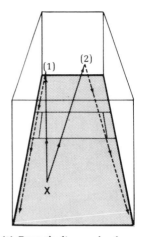

(1) Down-the-line overhead drive shot
(2) Cross-court overhead drive shot

either a cross-court, or a down-the-wall overhead may catch him off guard, since, up until the last moment, it looks like a regular ceiling shot.

The stroke is the same as is used for the forehand ceiling shot and overhead kill. The ball must hit the front wall 2–4 feet off the floor, and with enough speed to pass the opponent, or drive him deep into the back court. Novice players often make the mistake of hitting the front wall too high, so it is helpful to aim this shot at a spot which is about one foot above the floor. For the overhead drive to be successful, the ball should not bounce off the back wall so far that your opponent will have an easy setup. If the ball hits the sidewall, it should do so at a point at least three quarters of the way back from the front wall. Overall the overhead drive should be used more often across court than down the wall.

Back-into-back-wall shot

This defensive shot should be used in *emergencies only*, when no other shot is possible. The only time it is acceptable is when an opponent accurately hits a ball which goes past you, and does not carry all the way to the back wall. In order to keep the ball in play, your only choice is to hit the ball so it strikes the back wall first.

Hit the ball with a slight upward motion, either forehand or backhand. The closer you are to the back wall when executing this shot, the higher the ball should be hit on the back wall. The average shot strikes about 5 feet off the floor. Then the player must move himself out of the way immediately, since the rebound is instantaneous. The ball will travel from the back wall to a point high on the front wall, rebound to the floor near the front of the service area, and take a high, slow bounce back toward mid court.

Since this shot gives the opponent a very easy setup, the back-into-back wall should be used only as a last resort.

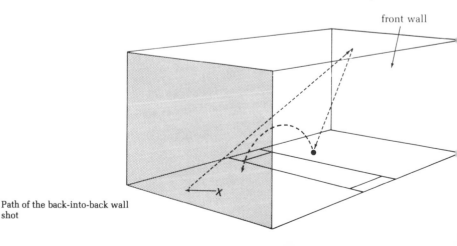

front wall

Path of the back-into-back wall shot

DRILLS

Racquetball players who wish to improve their skills should not only schedule their court time for actual game competition, but they should also allow adequate time for specific development drills. While games present unpredictable circumstances and require quick adjustments by the player, drills offer the opportunity to work repeatedly on the same stroke in a controlled stiuation. They are essential for establishing good forehand and backhand strokes. Effective responses to game situations may be practiced without the peculiar stresses of competition. Repetition of a shot will make a player comfortable with it, allowing him to relax and execute the shot properly in game situations. Drills are essential in developing touch, the ability to control the direction and the amount of force used in a shot. This is particularly important when attempting soft shots, such as the drop, the lob, and the lob serve.

There are two important points to remember when you are drilling: (1) In practicing a particular shot, drills of increasing difficulty should be used. (2) Drills designed to eliminate specific weaknesses, as well as those to develop specific strengths, should be included.

The table below shows the areas on the court from which various serves and shots should be practiced:

Serve	Court Area
hard drive	
three-quarter drive	
cross-court (including reverse, with variations, and high Z)	near middle of service area
low hard Z	
lob	
garbage	

Shot	
Offensive	
straight kill	middle and back
pinch kill	all
front wall–side wall kill	middle and back
overhead kill	back
down-the-line pass	all
cross-court pass	all
drop	front
Defensive	
ceiling	middle and back
Z	middle and back, some front
around-the-wall	middle and back
overhead drive	middle and back

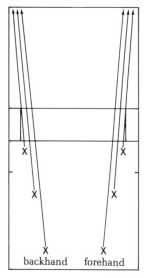

Drop and hit drill (hit from
three positions)

All the drills are to be practiced with both the forehand
and backhand strokes, using the forehand on the forehand
side of the court, and the backhand on the backhand side.
Drills for individual use will be described first, followed
by those which two players may practice together.

Forehand and backhand stroke drills

These drills will help the player practice the forehand and
backhand strokes, facilitate solid ball contact, and begin
to develop touch control.

Drop and hit   (1) Stand 3 feet from the side wall at the
short service line, face the side wall, drop the ball in front
of your body at arm's length, and hit it at knee height
against the front wall. The ball should contact the front
wall 3–5 feet above the floor, and rebound back to the
player. (2) After practicing from this position, move back
to the middle of the court, still 3 feet away from the side
wall, and repeat the drill. (3) Move back to within 5 feet
of the back wall, and repeat the drill again.

Executing the drop and hit drill

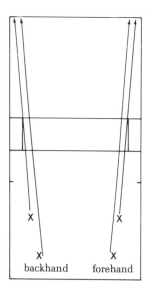

Setup and hit drill (hit from
two positions)

Setup and hit   This is a follow-up to the drop and hit
drill: (1) Hit an easy half-speed shot against the front wall.
(2) Then position yourself so you can step forward into
the rebound, and hit the ball at knee height against the
front wall again. Aim for front wall contact 3–5 feet above
the floor. (3) Perform this drill from the two positions
shown.

Forehand-backhand rally   This drill is particularly
good for perfecting grip changes on your racquet. (1) Hit
the ball against the front wall at moderate speed using

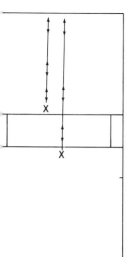

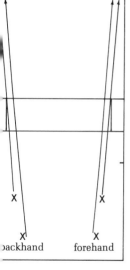

ehand-backhand rally drill
ernate hitting forehands and
khands from two positions in
court)

the forehand stroke. (2) After the ball rebounds, hit the ball with your backhand stroke against the front wall. (3) When the ball rebounds, hit the ball with the forehand. (4) Continue playing as long as you can alternate shots. Drill at a distance 10–15 feet from the front wall (front court), and also at 20–25 feet (center court).

Offensive shot drills

The following kill shot drills can be used for straight front wall kills, pinch kills (side wall–front wall) and front wall –side wall kills.

Drop and kill   (1) Repeat the drop and hit drill, only this time contact the ball at a point between your ankle and the top of your sock. Aim for a spot on the front wall which is only a couple of inches above the floor. (2) Practice from the 3 positions shown.

Setup and kill   (1) Repeat the setup and hit drill, but try to contact the ball at ankle height, aiming at a spot a few inches above the floor on the front wall. Concentrate on using the proper footwork. Practice from the 2 positions shown. (2) As an alternative exercise, stand at three-quarter court (in the middle), and hit a setup off the front wall. If the ball comes to your forehand side, hit a forehand to the forehand front corner. If it is on your backhand side, turn and hit a backhand kill shot.

backhand   forehand

p and kill drill

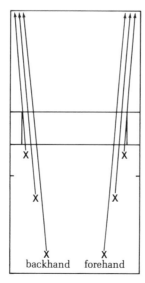

backhand   forehand

Setup and kill drill

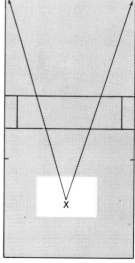

Setup and kill (alternate exercise)

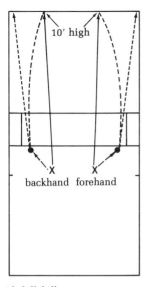

10' high

·X   X

backhand forehand

Fly kill drill

Fly kill   (1) Hit the ball approximately 10 feet hi
against the front wall. (2) Move to the rebounding b
and try to intercept it below waist level, before the b
hits the ground. (3) Kill the ball against the front w
(4) Practice from middle and back court.

Continuous lob and kill   (1) Hit a lob shot to the fr
wall. (2) After the ball bounces, try to make a low k
(3) When the ball comes back, lob it against the front w
again. (4) Keep the ball in play as long as you can by al
nating shots.

Overhead kill shot   The best way to practice the ov
head kill shot is to (1) hit a ceiling ball which rebounds i
the back court. (2) At shoulder level, hit the ball acr
court—into the opposite front corner, within a three-f
square.

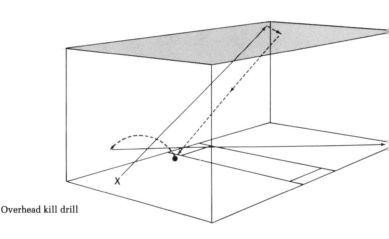

Overhead kill drill

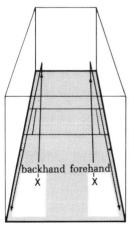

backhand forehand

X   X

Down-the-line pass drills: Drop
and hit and setup and hit

These two drills are used to practice down-the-line pa
shots:

Drop and hit   (1) Stand at three-quarter court, 3 f
from the side wall (2) drop the ball and contact it betwe
your knee and your waist, and hit a pass shot which
bounds off the front wall and travels along the side w
closest to you. (3) Hit the ball with topspin or backsp
so the ball will hug the side wall before dying in the r
corner.

Setup and hit   (1) Repeat the drop and hit drill p
cedures, only hit the pass shot as the ball rebounds of
front wall setup which you have executed. (2) Catch
ball in your hand, and repeat.

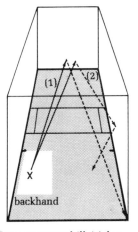

Cross-court pass drill: (1) drop
and hit (normal-angled pass)
(2) drop and hit (wider-angled
pass)

The following drills are valuable for practicing cross-court pass shots:

Drop and hit   (1) Stand at about two-thirds court, 3 feet from a side wall. (2) Drop the ball, contact it at knee height, and aim for the middle of the front wall, 3 feet above the floor. Hit the shot with approximately 80% of your most powerful effort. (3) Experiment with various angles, contacting the front wall at different spots.

Setup and hit   (1) Hit a setup off the front wall as you are standing at two-thirds court. Contact the ball at knee height, and aim for the middle of the front wall. (2) Move to the rebound and hit a cross-court pass. Vary the point of contact at the front wall so you hit variously angled cross-court pass shots. (3) Use a variety of setups: soft lobs, harder rebounds, short ceiling balls, and back wall setups.

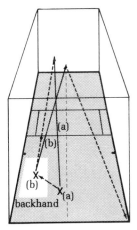

Cross-court pass drill: Setup
and hit
(a) Hit an easy setup against the
    front wall
(b) Move to the ball and hit a
    normal-angled cross-court
    pass

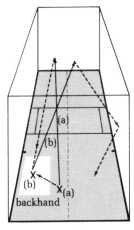

Cross-court pass drill: Setup
and hit
(a) Hit an easy setup against the
    front wall
(b) Move to the ball and hit a
    wider-angled cross-court
    pass

These exercises will help develop your back wall shots:

Toss and hit   (1) Stand 5 feet in front of the rear wall, face the side wall with your racquet in the ready position, and toss the ball against the back wall so it strikes about

5 feet above the floor. (2) As the ball rebounds off the back wall, move with it, using either the stop-and-step or jog and-hit method. (3) Contact the ball at knee height, o lower, and hit either a pass or kill shot. Concentrate o hitting the ball at a point adjacent to the lead foot.

Hard setup and hit   (1) Start at a position 4 feet awa from a side wall and 3 feet behind the short line. (2) H a setup off the front wall which rebounds at a moderat speed off the back wall, so the ball travels 4–7 feet out int the court. (3) As the ball travels toward the back wall, sid shuffle after it. Stop and reverse direction as the ball con tacts the back wall, step into it, and hit it against the fron wall. Use a pass or kill shot.

Soft setup and hit   This is the same exercise as th hard setup and hit except the rebound off the back wal should drop rapidly, instead of carrying, off the back wall To obtain this soft back wall rebound, lob the ball high, an gently, against the front wall. Since this exercise is harde to perform than the "hard setup and hit," the previous dril should be practiced before attempting it.

Back corner pickup   This drill is especially good fo players who have difficulty with their wrist snap, or get ting the ball out of the back corners.

(1) Gently toss the ball into one of the back corners so i hits the back wall, side wall, and then the floor. (2) Hit i so it strikes the front wall. (3) Start the drill with tosse which reach a height of 4 feet, and work down to the 1-foo level. At the 1-foot height, only a good wrist snap wil allow you to hit the ball all the way to the front.

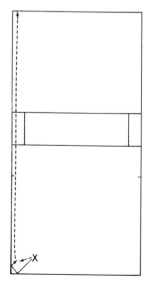

Executing the back wall toss and hit drill

Back corner pickup

Defensive shot drills

The ceiling shot is the most important of all defensive shots; it deserves the greatest proportion of defensive practice time. These drills will assist you in developing your shots which are directed toward the ceiling:

Drop and hit   (1) Stand in the backhand rear corner of the court, drop the ball, hit a backhand ceiling shot down the line, and catch the rebound. Contact the ball at a point between your waist and your shoulders. (2) Repeat until your stroke, and accuracy, are satisfactory. (3) Then go to the forehand rear corner, toss the ball up into the air, and hit a forehand ceiling ball down the line.

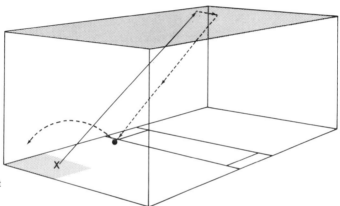

ling shot drill: drop and hit

Setup and hit   This is the same exercise as the drop and hit except that you must hit a soft setup to the front wall which rebounds to a rear corner, prior to hitting the ceiling ball. For both the backhand and forehand, hit the ball down the line. Additionally, on the forehand, direct some shots across court to the backhand rear corner.

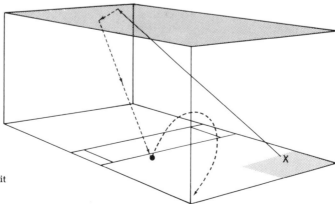

ling shot drill: setup and hit

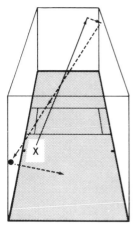

Backhand Z shot: drop and hit

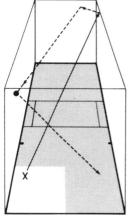

Around-the-wall shot drill:
drop and hit

Continuous ceiling shot   This is the most benefic[ial?]
defensive shot drill a player can practice alone. (1) Beg[in]
by hitting a ceiling ball on the backhand side. If the hit[is]
properly executed, the ball will rebound into the backha[nd]
rear corner where you must contact it, hitting another ce[il]ing ball. (2) Continue this rally of down-the-line backha[nd]
ceiling balls until a mistake is made. Try to make each sh[ot]
hug the side wall, and carry deep into the back court.
Repeat this same drill on the forehand side.

The following drills will polish your Z ball shot ski[ll]

Drop and hit   (1) Stand just behind the service b[ox?]
near a side wall, and drop the ball. (2) Hit it upward, a[nd]
across court, against the front wall. Aim for a spot 3 f[eet]
below the ceiling, and 3 feet away from the side wall.

Setup and hit   Follow the same procedures as th[ose]
in the drop and hit exercise, except first hit a soft set[up]
off the front wall before trying the Z shot. Concentr[ate]
on contacting the ball at waist level.

Around-the-wall shot drills:

Drop and hit   (1) Position yourself in the back cou[rt]
on the backhand side. (2) Drop the ball and hit a backha[nd]
around-the-wall shot which strikes the forehand side w[all]
first. (3) Continue this for awhile, and then begin to [hit]
forehand around-the-wall shots from the same positi[on]
against the same spot on the forehand side wall. (4) N[ow]
move to the forehand side of the back court, and make[a]
forehand around-the-wall shot which initially strikes t[he]
backhand wall.

Setup and hit   This is the same drill as the drop a[nd]
hit, only the around-the-wall shot is hit after a soft set[up]
is made off the front wall.

Ceiling shot setup and hit   Again, this exercise [is]
identical to the setup and hit, but the around-the-w[all]
shot is hit after a ceiling ball setup is made.

The best way to practice the overhead drive shot is[:]
(1) stand in a rear corner and (2) hit a ceiling ball whi[ch]
returns to you at shoulder height, or above. (3) Then [hit]
this high rebound against the front wall, using your dri[ve.]
Hit the ball either across court, or down the line. Y[ou]
should direct your shot so it strikes a spot on the fr[ont]
wall which is three feet above the ground. The play[er]
should remember to aim lower than he believes necessa[ry]
as the ball tends to contact the front wall higher th[an]

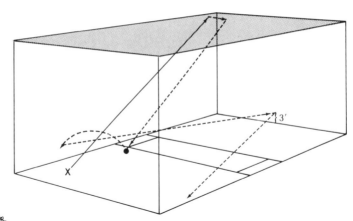

ss-court overhead drive
t drill

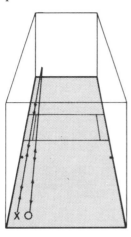

intended. Avoid causing the ball to strike the back wall too hard on its final rebound. Also be careful not to let it pop off the side wall in the front three quarters of the court.

Drills for two players

While individual drills serve as the basis for perfecting most racquetball techniques, there may be times when you would prefer to practice with a partner. Try to find one whose abilities are similar to yours, and who understands that the particular court session is for drills, rather than games. Some specific partner routines are:

Perpetual pass shot   Using the down-the-line or cross-court pass drill, each player acts as a mutual ball returner, alternating turns hitting the ball. A perpetual drive pass rally is essentially what occurs. Both players should strive for control, rather than trying to hit the ball past each other.

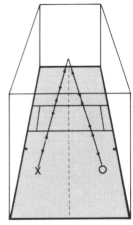

Perpetual down-the-line pass
drill with two players

Perpetual cross-court pass drill
with two players

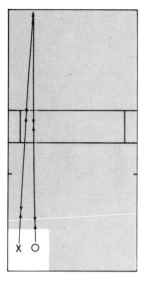

Perpetual backhand ceiling ball drill with two players

Perpetual ceiling ball To practice down-the-li ceiling shots, both players must alternate hitting ceili balls to each other, near both the backhand and foreha side walls. This is probably the best defensive drill t can be performed with two people.

In order to practice the cross-court ceiling shot, positi one player in the backhand rear corner and the other the forehand rear corner. Alternate hitting ceiling ba across court to each other. One player should be hitti mostly backhands and the other mostly forehands, so po tions should be exchanged occasionally to give the play a workout using each stroke. If the players make a rig and left-handed combination, this drill is especially be ficial when both of them are stationed in spots whi facilitate a continuous backhand rally.

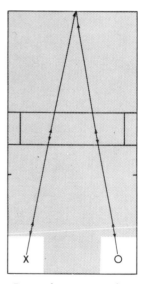

Perpetual cross-court ceiling ball drill with two players

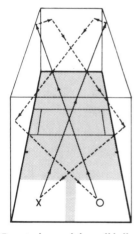

Perpetual around-the-wall ball drill with two players

Perpetual around-the-wall ball To practice t shot, station one player on the deep forehand side of t court, and the other on the deep backhand side. Ea player alternates hitting around-the-wall balls using eit a backhand or forehand stroke. Ideally, after some practi each shot will end up deep in the rear corner, makin return shot very difficult. The players should switch si occasionally.

SINGLES STRATEGY

The player with sound strokes is at a distinct advantage in a racquetball match, but without a set of strategies to complement them the competitor is sorely unequipped. *Strategy* is essentially a plan for obtaining a specific goal or result. In racquetball as in other sports where the objective is to win a game or match, good strategy involves assessing the strengths and weaknesses of all players in order to take advantage of your own strengths while capitalizing on your opponent's weaknesses. If your advantages outnumber those of your opponent, then you are playing "percentage racquetball," and, most likely, a winning singles game. The first step in acquiring an understanding of strategy is to familiarize yourself with its two basic elements: court position and shot selection.

1. Court position

From the center court position a player can control pla[...]
A large number of your opponent's shots can be retrieve[...]
and a greater selection of shots can be executed, with mo[...]
ease, than from any other court location. In fact, cent[...]
court has enough swinging room to allow you to hit eve[...]
racquetball shot, except those directly off the back wa[...]
Essentially, this position encompasses an area that is o[...]
or two steps behind the short line, approximately equ[...]
distant from any two corresponding points on the court

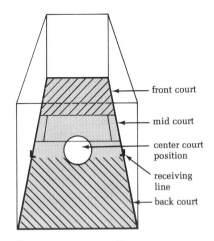

front court

mid court

center court
position

receiving
line

back court

Proper center court position

Within the general center court area, a player's actu[...]
position is determined by the game situation (i.e., wheth[...]
he has just served, hit a ceiling ball, hit a weak shot, [...]
tempted a kill, etc.). Most players, and beginners in part[...]
ular, play too close to the front wall. This is not necessa[...]
since most of their opponent's shots will hit high on t[...]
front wall, and into the back court. Advanced play[...]
have no need to play close to the front wall since they c

Watching a return from the
center court position

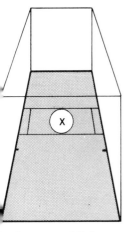

st players, especially be-
ners, play too close to the
ht wall, leaving most of the
rt unprotected

anticipate an opponent's shots well enough to cover the front court shots from the center court position. Also, from center court, the player is daring an opponent to hit a kill shot—which is usually hit high. Since it is easier to move forward to a ball than backward, the player in center court is in the right place to move forward and retrieve the attempted kill.

A good example of the value of center court positioning follows: A player finds himself standing in the back court, having just made a weak shot which bounds into mid court. In this situation, most beginners will make the mistake of either rushing up to the short line to cover the opponent's possible kill shot, or staying back to retrieve a pass shot. The best court coverage in this situation requires two movements: (a) running to the center court area, and, (b) as the opponent swings at the ball, determining if the shot will be a kill or pass, and covering accordingly. If the player cannot tell what kind of shot his opponent is making, he must make a guess and react, rather than standing flatfooted at center court. By making these two movements, not only is the player able to cover most shots, but he can also avoid committing himself too soon. The opponent will not be able to tell where the player is covering, prior to hitting his shot.

WRONG MOVE	WRONG MOVE	RIGHT MOVE

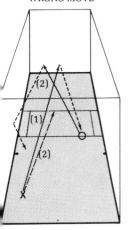

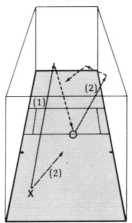

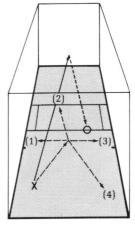

Player O receives an easy setup
Player O hits a cross-court pass by player X who is charging too far forward in anticipation of a kill shot attempt

(1) Player O receives an easy setup
(2) Player O hits a pinch kill which player X cannot reach because he has only moved to cover a pass shot attempt

Covering a setup—use two motions:
First run to center court
Then move to another position to intercept opponent's shot:

1 to intercept cross-court pass

2 to intercept pinch shot

3 to intercept straight kill

4 to intercept down-the-line pass

2. Shot selection

Proper shot selection is the "first mate" of proper co
position. The correct shot will allow you to attain a
maintain the center court spot. Many variables come i,
play when choosing a particular shot: the opponer
abilities, the score, initial court position, etc.

Both basic elements of strategy—court position and s⟋
selection—will be elaborated upon in the following c
cussions.

Beginning tactics

A racquetball *beginner* is a player who has trouble c⟋
trolling almost every shot. Since even hitting the ball
a straight line can be troublesome for the beginner, t⟋
player's particular strategy should be oriented towa
basic control during rallies. The keys to this control a⟋

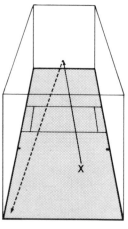

Beginning Tactic: Hit all shots
cross-court, deep into the corner.
Try not to hit the side walls

a) *Ball control.* Concentrate on bringing the racq⟋
back to an early set position. Try to meet the bal⟋
waist level, or below.

b) *Center court position.* While playing, concentr⟋
on your court position more than on the particu⟋
of shot execution, which should have been practic⟋
during drills.

c) *Shot selection.* Attempt to hit all shots across co⟋
into the back corner, without hitting the side wa⟋
This maneuver will prevent your opponent fr⟋
receiving too many easy setups in mid court, a⟋
will cause him to work harder.

d) *Serve selection.* When serving, meet the ball
front of your body. Choose serves that will go int⟋
back corner of the court.

e) *Serve return.* Try to develop consistency by retu⟋
ing all of your opponent's serves with the same sh⟋
Ideally, try to place this shot into the back court⟋

After learning these strategies the beginner will find t⟋
his mind is relatively free of technicalities, allowing h⟋
to concentrate on his overall basic game. Once the begin⟋
becomes more proficient at hitting balls that die in
back corners, he should progress to intermediate strate⟋

Intermediate tactics

An *intermediate* player possesses the basic skills wh⟋
allow him to hit all shots fairly well in practice, but ha⟋
harder time in game situations, when easy shots do ⟋
always appear. Intermediate strategy should incorpor⟋
two principles:

a) A player's best shots should be emphasized.

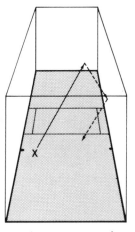

Intermediate Tactic: Do not hit
shots which rebound off the side
wall into center court

b) Shots should be chosen which will minimize the points a player will lose, and which will also put the most pressure on the opponent.

In general, the intermediate player should practice patience during rallies, and wait for an opportunity to make a kill shot—one which the player is confident can be executed very accurately. On service returns, the player should use ceiling ball shots, rather than try for kills. On all front- and mid-court setups. kill shots should be attempted, whether the player is proficient at them or not. On the other hand, back court kill attempts should not be made until the player has adequately developed them.

A common error is to make a shot which rebounds off the side wall, straight through center court. This will give the opponent the center court position, and an easy setup. If you study the following specific situations, you may be able to avoid similar mistakes, and at the same time learn more about intermediate tactics.

Opponent in center court, Player in front   If you should find that your opponent is behind you during a game, you should attempt a kill shot which initially hits the front wall at a point 5–6 feet from the side wall. As the player becomes more proficient at keeping the ball off the side wall, this distance may be reduced. If it is an accurate kill, your opponent's chances of reaching it are slim. Even if your shot is hit too high, the ball will rebound into the back court along the side wall, forcing the opponent out of the center.

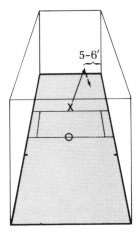

Intermediate Tactic: (Opponent
in center court, player in front)
Path of a good kill shot

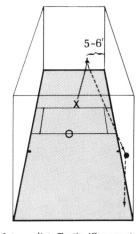

Intermediate Tactic: (Opponent
in center court, player in front)
Path of a kill shot which hits the
front wall too high, travels into
the back court, but still is effective

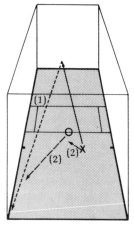

Intermediate Tactic: (Opponent in center court, player in back)
(1) Hit a pass shot to the opponent's backhand
(2) As the opponent O moves to retrieve the shot, player X must also move to center court to be in proper position to intercept O's return

The advantages of this tactic are:

a) The opponent's view is partially obstructed by th player.

b) The opponent must contend with a ball that is trave ing close to the side wall.

c) Even if the kill is not executed properly, and th ball takes a route through center court, it is usuall traveling too fast for your opponent to make an effe(tive return.

d) The worst thing that can happen is that a hinde may be called on you for hitting the ball back 1 yourself.

Opponent in center court, Player in back   In thi situation, a pass shot to the opponent's weak side (no) mally the backhand) is a good idea. The player shoul move to center court as soon as the opponent is forced t relinquish his position. If the player's pass shots are n(effectively forcing the opponent out of center court, the he should try ceiling shots.

Advanced tactics

By the time a player reaches the advanced level, he wi already be able to execute all shots well—not only i practice, but also in game situations. In order to becom consistently successful, the advanced player should con centrate on gaining a thorough knowledge of the situation where particular shots should be used. These situation can be grouped into four strategic categories:

a) Serve strategy

b) Serve return strategy

c) Serve return coverage strategy

d) Rally strategy

Each particular group of strategies, and the shots whic are used with them, will be discussed in detail.

Serve strategy

The easiest way to gain center court position is to win rally and earn the serve. Since most serves originate fro the middle of the service area, the server begins play in position which is only one or two steps forward of cent(court, and equidistant from both side walls, while th opponent is deep in the back court. Good serve strateg is designed so the server maintains this center court pos tion: By careful serve selection, the player can force th desired type of return from his opponent.

Low serves, such as the drive and low Z, are used to pr(duce weak returns. Higher serves, like the garbage, lob, an high Z, are handy when a service error cannot be afforde(

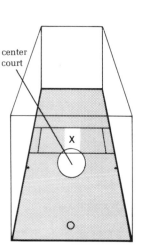

Serve strategy: If the serve is made from the middle of the service box, the server can easily move into the center court position

They also limit the opponent's choice of returns. In general, low zone serves are more effective, but harder to control.

An opponent should initially be tested with different serves, hit at various speeds. Once a weakness has been found (and it usually is in the opponent's backhand) take advantage of it with the proper serve. The player must also consider his preferred style of play, and serve accordingly. If, for example, the player likes to return ceiling balls, then a high serve to the opponent will usually force this kind of shot from him. If aggressive front court play is preferred, try to make your opponent kill the ball while still keeping the percentages in your favor. A serve directed to waist level may accomplish this, since it is a hard shot to kill, and yet a very enticing one for an impatient opponent.

In keeping with the basic fundamentals of service strategy, you should:

a) Vary serves. Keep your opponent guessing.
b) Hit different serves from the same service area. Concentrate on showing your opponent the same foot position, ball drop, and arm motion for various types of serves.
c) Quickly move back to center court if you have served from a point a step or two to the left or right of it.
d) Avoid serving the ball so hard that it rebounds strongly off the back wall, giving the receiver an easy shot.
e) Try to direct serves so they travel close to the side walls, and deep into the back corners.

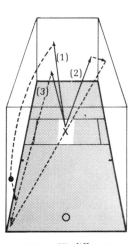

Serve strategy: Hit different serves from the same service area:
1) Lob serve
2) Low Z serve
3) Drive serve

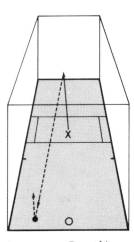

Serve strategy: Do not hit serves that rebound strongly off the back wall

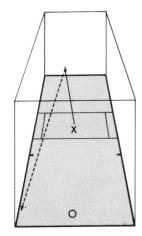

Serve strategy: Hit serves close to the side walls, and deep into the back corners

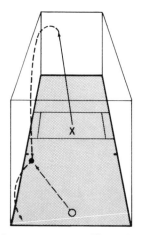

Serve return strategy: The service receiver should move up and take all high serves on the fly before the ball hits the floor. Do not wait for the ball to go into the deep back court before hitting it

Serve return strategy

When awaiting a serve from your opponent, you shoul stand in a position slightly within the backhand cour Since the server's center court position gives him an initia advantage, the primary objective of the service return to take the center away from him. The serve returne should remember to:

a) Move up and hit all high serves on the fly, if possibl This shot does not have to be perfect, since the serve will usually be unprepared for it.

b) Try to "read" the serve. Watch for any idiosyncr sies the server may reveal, and where he contac the ball. You may be able to tell whether the serv is coming high or low.

c) Try to hit an offensive shot on all serves taken belo the knees, a defensive shot on all those above kne level.

There are four primary serve returns which will enab the player who has lost the serve and center court pos tion to regain them: the ceiling shot, the cross-court driv pass, the down-the-line drive pass, and the around-th wall shot. Three other returns, the kill shot, Z ball, and lo are possible but not as effective. The lob is not recom mended for use on serve returns, except as a last reso Remember that over 90 percent of all serves are directed the backhand corner; the main emphasis while practicir serve return shots should be on this side.

Ceiling return   This is the safest serve return. Co sequently, it is the one used most often during a matc The shot does not have to be hit perfectly in order to effective, and it can be used to return any kind of serv It will immediately drive the server into the back court

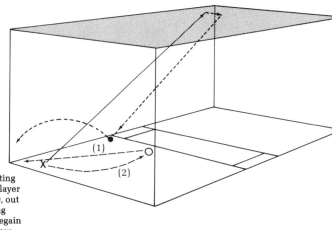

Serve return strategy: By hitting a ceiling ball serve return, player X forces the server, player O, out of center court position along path (1). Player X will then regain center court position by follow- ing path (2)

chase of the ball, allowing the serve returner to regain center court.

When the ceiling shot is executed properly, the ball will rebound deep into the left or right half of the court, ideally along the side wall on the server's backhand side. In this situation, it will be extremely difficult for your opponent to hit an offensive shot: His only choice is to hit another ceiling ball. At this point neither player will have an advantage, so the ceiling ball rally should be continued until your opponent makes a mistake, allowing you to gain the center court position.

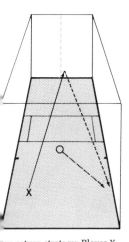

ve return strategy: Player X s a cross-court drive pass serve urn (slightly to the right of ter on the front wall) which ounds into the deep right-rear ner. Player O, the server, is ced out of center court posi- n to retrieve the ball

Hitting a ceiling ball serve return

Cross-court drive pass return   Although this may be the easiest serve return to execute, proper ball placement is essential. The ball should hit the front wall slightly to the right of center if the serve has been directed to the left back corner; slightly to the left if it comes to the right corner. It must be hit with enough force to drive it past the server, so he has to leave center court to make a retrieve.

The cross-court drive return is most advantageously used against:

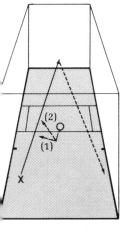

ve return strategy: The best es to hit a cross-court pass are: If the server is leaning toward the side of the court from which he served If the server is moving for- ward in anticipation of a kill shot return

a) Ill-placed garbage serves which pop off the side wall in shallow back court, or carry off the back wall.

b) Low, hard drive serves which wrap around the rear corner, making a good setup, or which rebound straight off the back wall.

c) Any serve which comes to the forehand below the waist (provided that the player has enough time to set himself).

This return is especially effective if the server is moving toward the front court, anticipating a kill service return. It should also be used if the server is leaning toward the side of the court to which he served.

The main problems associated with this service retu
are:

a) If the server is quick on his feet, and anticipates t
   return shot, he will easily step into the cross-co
   lane and kill the ball into the front wall corner (s
   diagram below).

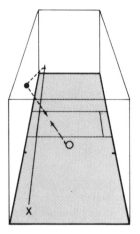

Serve return strategy: If a down-
the-wall pass return hits the side
wall in front of mid court, the
ball will rebound into mid court
for an easy play by the server

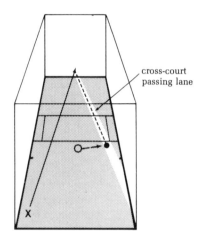

cross-court
passing lane

b) If the cross-court pass is hit too hard, the ball w
   rebound off the back wall, making an easy setup
   the server.

c) If the cross-court pass is hit against the front w
   too wide, the ball will rebound off the side wa
   giving your opponent an easy shot.

Down-the-wall drive pass return   This serve retu
is a difficult shot to control, but very effective when pr
erly hit. The ball is returned along the side wall, on t
same side in which the serve was received. Hopeful
it will rebound back along the side wall without touchi
it (at least not until it reaches the back court). If the b
does hit the side wall before it reaches this point, it w
either rebound into center court, making an easy sett
or it will lose enough speed to allow the server to rea
it. This return must be hit hard to keep the server fre
intercepting it at mid court.

The best situations in which to use this return are:

a) When the server is standing on the opposite side
   the court from the receiver.

b) When the server is creeping toward the corner of t
   front wall which is located on the same side of t
   court as the receiver.

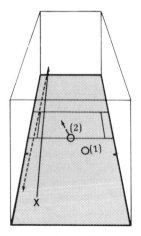

Serve return strategy: Hit a down-
the-line pass return: (1) when the
server is standing on the opposite
side of the court from the ball; (2)
if the server is edging toward the
front wall on the serve reception
side

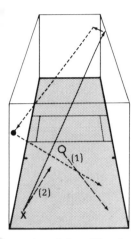

Serve return strategy: When the serve returner, player X, hits an around-the-wall ball, the server, player O, is forced out of center court along path (1). Player X can then assume center court by moving along path (2)

Like the aforementioned service returns, an effective down-the-wall pass will force the server to give up the center court during his attempt to retrieve the ball.

Around-the-wall return   This service return is particularly potent against beginning and intermediate players. It is used primarily as a change of pace shot, alternating with ceiling ball returns. The around-the-wall return is used to best advantage against "soft" serves (garbage, high Z, and lob). It is used frequently on the backhand side of the court, causing the ball eventually to end up in the rear forehand corner.

Kill return   This service return should be attempted only when a poor serve has given the receiver enough time, and room, to set up for a good shot. Although it will keep the server on his toes, the odds on this shot are against the serve returner: If the ball hits the floor before reaching the front wall, the server has gained an easy point; if it hits the front wall too high, it will give the server his own easy kill shot.

A majority of these returns should be directed into the front wall corner that is located on the same side of the court as the serve was initially placed. This will keep the distance the ball has to travel to a minimum, and thus allow the serve returner the best chance of making a good shot.

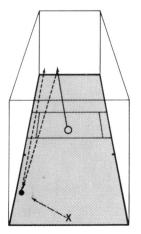

Serve return strategy: On a kill shot serve return, direct the shot into the front wall corner on the side of the court on which the serve is placed

---

Common faults (Serve return)

1 *After hitting the service return, the player does not move into the center court position.*

2 *The player does not choose his serve returns carefully, but sprays shots at random.*

3 *The player forgets that the prime objective is to take away the server's positional advantage.*

4 *The player "runs around" a serve directed to the backhand side, attempting to hit it with his forehand.*

5 *The player does not use the ceiling return enough.*

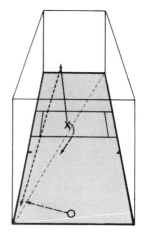

After serving, the server should retreat on a diagonal toward the rear corner where the serve was directed

Covering the service return

Returning to the server's vantage point, it is now necessary to examine the ways in which he can maintain his positional advantage after he has served. After hitting the serve, the server should:

a) Drop back diagonally toward the rear corner where the serve was directed. The distance of the retreat depends on the accuracy of the serve. (Retreat 4 or 5 steps on a good garbage serve, and 0–2 steps on a bad drive serve.)

b) Look over the shoulder, and turn the body toward the ball slightly, in order to get an indication of what type of return the opponent will hit.

c) Hold the racquet in the ready position, body bent forward slightly, ready to move.

The player should position himself just outside, or inside the *hitting area*. This is the area where an offensive service return is likely to be directed. It is determined by drawing imaginary lines from the front wall corners to the spot where the server expects the returned ball to be contacted. The better his serve, the further the server should move into the hitting area, since he may be able to force a return down the wall. By moving into this area, the player cuts off many possible avenues of return. Down-the-wall and cross-court shots (which are not kills) often become setups as long as the player remains in front of the opponent. Care must be taken, however, not to move so far into the hitting area as to block the opponent's shot, thus creating an avoidable hinder.

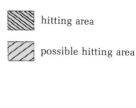

hitting area

possible hitting area

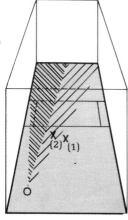

Court position after the serve:
(1) The server is standing just outside the hitting area
(2) The server is standing just inside the hitting area

ering the service return

The most important rule to remember is to keep your eyes on the ball at all times. If you don't, you will have no idea where your opponent is attempting to place the return, and consequently you will have difficulty getting ready to hit your next shot.

Specific defenses the player can use against serve returns will now be examined:

Ceiling shot defense   If the server is driven out of center court by a ceiling ball return, there is very little he can do to regain his position other than to hit another ceiling ball. Other types of shots will usually fail to move the opponent: A kill attempt from deep back court will usually fail; a Z-ball return takes a tremendous amount of power and good timing; and a pass shot usually will not have enough speed on it to "pass" the opponent.

The ceiling shot should be directed to the opponent's backhand.

Cross-court pass defense   When defending against a cross-court pass return, the server must try to anticipate the path that the opponent's shot will take off the front wall. If the pass return is executed correctly this job is relatively simple, since there is only one path the ball can take. This path is called the *passing lane,* and it is approximately two feet in width.

To defend against the cross-court serve return, the server must move into the passing lane and kill the ball in the nearest front wall corner, using a short, firm stroke. If a fly kill is attempted, the wrist should not snap prior to ball contact. If the server feels the opponent is charging in to cover his kill shot attempt, a cross-court pass should be used.

e the serve returner has hit a
ss-court pass, the server must
ve to the passing lane (white
a) and hit a kill shot into the
rest front wall corner (a). If
serve returner charges
vard anticipating the kill
t, hit a cross-court pass (b)

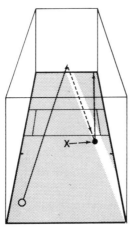

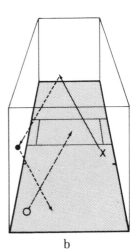

a   b

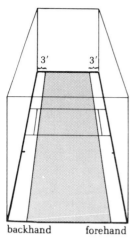

backhand   forehand

Down-the-wall passing lanes

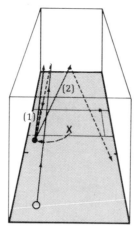

← Down-the-wall pass defense: As the serve returner hits a down-the-wall pass, the server steps into the passing lane and hits either (1) a kill shot to the nearest corner or (2) a cross-court pass

Down-the-wall pass defense   If the serve return directed down the wall, again the server must cover passing lane. In this instance the lane encompasses an a about three feet wide. The server should be able to ant pate this shot, especially on a backhand serve return, si most such returns will be along the same side of the co as the serve. Once in the lane, the server can either the ball into the nearest front wall corner, or hit a cr court pass shot.

Kill shot defense   As soon as the server sees that opponent's return is going to be a kill, the player m get set for it. If the kill shot is a roll-out, there is noth the player can do; there is no defense against it. But if

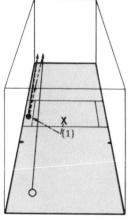

After serving, player X must move up and over from center court position at (1) to intercept a kill shot service return and rekill the ball

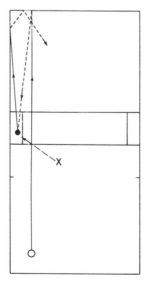

The server, player X, in covering opponent O's kill shot service return attempt, hits a pinch shot rekill

The server, while covering a shot service return, reaches t ball and hits a front wall-side wall rekill

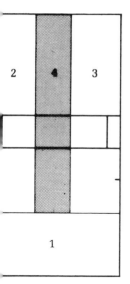

kill is high, the player has time to move forward and re-kill the ball into the same corner. A short, quick stroke should be used for speed and accuracy. In this instance power can be sacrificed for accuracy—although the shot does not have to be as accurate as the opponent's original kill serve return. The most effective re-kills are the pinch kill (side wall-front wall), and the front wall-side wall kill.

Rally strategy

If the service, the return, or the shot covering the service return, has not ended play, a *rally* is in progress. The specific strategy a player now uses to win the point depends upon his general court position. Keeping this in mind, you should apply two basic rules during rallies:

a) Use complementary shots. For example, if one of your shots forces your opponent forward, and to the left side of the court, hit your next shot deep to the right side.

b) Apply offensive and defensive concepts. In the front court hit offensive shots, in mid court play aggressively, and in the back court use defensive shots.

shot hitting areas—If you are
ted in the:
backcourt, do not attempt a
kill shot with your opponent
in the center court position
eft side court, direct most
kills to left front corner
·ight side court, direct most
kills to right front corner
shaded area, direct kills to
either front corner

Some general guidelines are summed up below and illustrated on the left.

ponent is in front court:

Player is in front court	Pass. *Do not attempt a kill shot.*
Player is in mid court or back court	Pass; hit a ceiling shot, Z shot, or around-the-wall shot. *Do not attempt a kill shot.*

ponent is in mid court:

Player is in front court	Pass; hit a drop shot, pinch kill, or Z ball.
Player is in mid court	Hit a pinch kill, front wall–side wall kill, cross-court pass, or ceiling shot.
Player is in back court	Hit a cross-court pass, ceiling shot, Z shot, or around-the-wall ball. Pinch kill occasionally.

ponent is in back court:

Player is in front court	Hit a drop shot, straight kill, pinch kill, or front wall–side wall kill. *Do not attempt a pass shot.*
Player is in mid court or back court	Hit a straight kill, pinch kill, front wall–side wall kill, or ceiling shot. *Do not attempt a pass shot.*

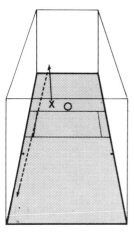

Player X and opponent in front court: Player X should hit a pass shot to the side of the court opposite the opponent

Front court position　The rally strategies used by player in the front court (the area between the front wa and the service line) depend on the location of the opp nent. However, the most commonly used shots are t pinch kill, drop shot, and pass. Following are some sp cific front-court rally situations and the best strategies each:

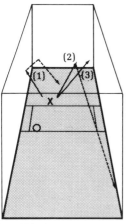

a) *Player and opponent in front court.* In this situati a player has only to hit a passing shot by the o ponent for a winner. Care must be taken, howeve not to hit the ball so hard that it reaches and bounds off the back wall. Hit the pass to the side the court away from the opponent.

b) *Player in left front court; opponent in mid court b tween left side wall and the player.* Try a pinch k to the left side, a cross-court pass deep to the rig back corner, or a drop shot to the right side. T opponent will not have time to retrieve any of the shots, all of which are traveling away from him.

c) *Player in front court; opponent in back court.* In t situation any kill or drop shot attempt is warrante The opponent is too deep to retrieve the ball befc the second bounce. A pass should not be used, the opponent is deep enough to cut off the bal path to a rear corner. The player should place t kill or drop shot on the side of the court nearest hi

Player X in front court, opponent in mid court: Try a pinch kill (1), cross-court pass to the right side (2), or a drop shot away from the opponent (3)

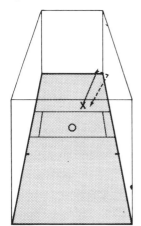

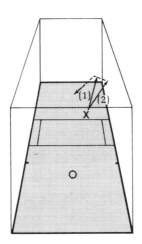

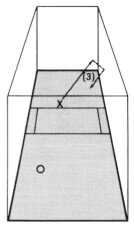

Player X in front court, opponent in mid court: If player X hits a poor front wall-side wall kill, he may be in the path of the ball, causing a hinder

Player X in front court, opponent in back court: Hit a straight kill or drop shot (1), pinch kill (2), or front wall–side wall kill (3)

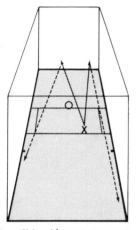

ayer X in mid court, opponent
front: Hit a pass shot, either
oss-court or down-the-line

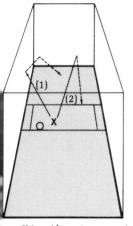

ayer X in mid court, opponent
one side: Hit a pinch kill
ot to the side wall nearest the
ponent (1) or a straight front
all kill or pass shot to the side
posite the opponent (2)

Middle court position   The middle court area (between the service and receiving lines) is the best location from which to control a rally. Here a player can choose from a wide selection of shots, especially offensive ones, and have an excellent chance of capitalizing on them. Coverage of the opponent's shots is now optimized because the player has relatively easy access to all surrounding court areas and has but to take a step or two to reach any ball the opponent hits, unless it is a good kill shot.

Aggressive, offensive play should be practiced. Hit kill shots into the front wall corners, and pass shots that force your opponent to the edges of center court. Cut off all pass attempts and volley every ball that comes at waist height or below. Several situations that may arise are:

a) *Player in middle court; opponent in front.* Hit a pass shot which is aimed toward the left or right, depending on the opponent's specific position. The opponent will not have enough time to react to cut off the pass shot. A kill shot is not a good shot selection unless you are presented with a perfect setup.

b) *Player in middle court; opponent on either side.*

c) *Player in middle court; opponent behind.* Try a kill shot into the front corner, away from the opponent. This play carries little risk of failure: If the ball rolls out, the player has scored a point or side out. If it rebounds out of the corner at a height where the opponent would normally be able to cover it, the player will be blocking the opponent's vision, or path, and a hinder must be called. In this case the player has lost nothing; the rally must be replayed. Furthermore, the natural tendency for an opponent, when he is forced to cover the kill shot, is to hang back in anticipation of a cross-court kill or pass. This action will leave him vulnerable to the corner kill.

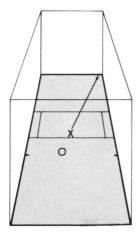

Player X in mid court, opponent
behind: Hit a kill shot to the
front wall corner, away from

Back court position   The back court (between the r͏eceiving line and back wall) is where most tactical mistake occur. While rallying in this area, a player can keep h͏is errors at a minimum by:

a) Playing defensively to avoid allowing the oppone͏nt court position or a setup.

b) Formulating a plan to get into offensive positio͏n and to this end constantly thinking out the best sh͏ot to use in each situation.

c) Keeping cool and watchful, ready to capitalize ͏at once on the opponent's first error.

d) Generally hitting the ball to the opponent's wea͏k side.

The ceiling shot should be relied upon in this particula͏r rally situation. It does not score many points by itself, bu͏t if you hit several of them your opponent may eventuall͏y make an error. Be careful not to have the ball hit the sid͏e wall too close to the front wall, or it will lead to an eas͏y setup for your opponent. After hitting the ceiling sho͏t take a position which is about halfway between the sho͏rt line and the back wall, edging a step toward the side wa͏ll.

A poorly hit ceiling ball which hits the side wall too close to the front wall gives opponent O an easy setup, either a kill shot (1) or a cross-court pass (2)

After hitting a good ceiling shot, player X must remember to return to proper center court position—halfway between the short line and back wall, and a step toward the side wall where the ball is traveling. By doing this, you will already be only a few steps away from the correct retrieval position should your opponent hit a return ceiling ball. If he tries an overhead kill, you must move forward *with* the shot, not before.

Another shot that is valuable during rallies in which the player finds himself in the back court is the kill. It should be used to earn the respect of the opponent, and must only be executed when the player has full confidence in it. If this shot is chosen the player should not make the mistake of standing still after the kill is made. The correct follow-up is to move immediately to center court, for a possible return shot. By doing this, the player will discourage the opponent from making a re-kill; if he does decide to make one, it will have to be very accurate. The kill shot should never be attempted, however, when the opponent is in front or mid court.

Other defensive shots that can be effective from the back court are the Z ball and the overhead drive pass, directed either across court or down the wall. Although the ceiling ball is more consistently successful, these shots make good changes of pace. Both of them give the player time to regain center court position before the opponent can hit a return. The overhead pass will work best when the opponent is in the vicinity of the back court, anticipating a ceiling ball return. If he is on the same side of the court as the player who is making the shot, a cross-court overhead pass should be used. If he is on the opposite side of the court, a down-the-wall overhead pass is the best choice.

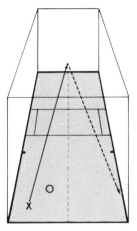

Both player X and opponent O in the backcourt, on the same side of the court: Hit a cross-court overhead drive pass if the opponent is anticipating a ceiling ball

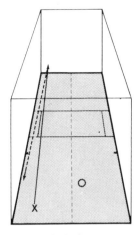

Player X in the backcourt, opponent O in the backcourt on the other side: Hit a down-the-wall overhead drive pass

DOUBLES STRATEGY

A person who does well at singles does not necessaril[y] make a good doubles player. Doubles racquetball is a mo[re] complex game, requiring more racquet control, patienc[e] and strategy. Each player is only one half of a team, a[nd] success in doubles depends on effective teamwork. Tea[m]mates must cooperate, learn each other's strengths a[nd] weaknesses, and enjoy playing together.

While the shots are the same for both singles and double[s] the presence of four players on the court significantly [re]duces the amount of unoccupied space. It is much hard[er] to "put the ball away," so rallies tend to last longer. T[he] most successful method of play is a patient, waiting gam[e.] A typical sight in doubles is an extended ceiling ball ral[ly] which eventually leads to a poorly hit ceiling shot, fo[l]lowed by a kill shot attempt, and perhaps a re-kill. Ea[ch] offensive shot must be a "winner"; otherwise the opposi[ng] team will probably capitalize on it.

Court position

Just as in singles play, it is advantageous for a team to [try] to dominate center court. Offensively, kill and pass sho[ts] are used most effectively from this position; defensivel[y] the players can easily move back to cover the opposi[ng] team's back-wall shots, or move forward to pick up th[eir] kill attempts. With both teams attempting to domin[ate] the important center court area, the game can sometim[es] become a fierce physical contest; therefore, it must [be] remembered that if one team is about to hit a shot, t[he] other team has an unwritten right to occupy center co[urt] position.

In order for a team to maximize court coverage in doubl[es] the two team members should "divide" the court betwe[en] themselves. There are two primary methods to acco[m]plish this: the side by side method, and the front and ba[ck] method.

Side by side method   This is the most commonl[y] used approach. Imagine the court divided in half by a li[ne] running from the front wall to the back wall. Each play[er] has one side of the court to cover; the players must deci[de] between themselves which side each will take:

a) If both players are right-handed or both are left-hand[ed] the player with the best backhand shot should be plac[ed] on the backhand side of the court. The player playing [in] this half will probably see the most action, since the o[p]posing team is likely to direct most of their shots his wa[y.] Besides taking the balls which come to the backhand h[alf] of the court, he should also take most of the shots hit do[wn]

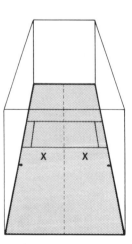

Side by side method of doubles
court coverage

the middle, as they will be to his forehand—if not, his teammate will have to hit a more difficult backhand shot.

The forehand partner must remember not to stand too close to the side wall, or he will be forced to use his backhand too often. He should concentrate on hitting forehand shots. During the course of the game, he will usually end up hitting more kill and pass shots than his backhand partner.

Occasionally both players will have to trade sides if one partner is temporarily caught out of position and unable to cover his territory. A switch back to their normal positions should be made as soon as possible:

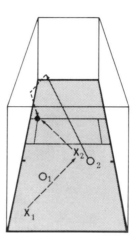

Doubles position strategy: Opponent O_2 hits a ball into player X_1's territory which partner X_2 must cover. Player X_1 then moves to cover X_2's territory

b) If one player is right-handed and the other left-handed, they should be positioned so both can execute forehand shots in the middle of the court, or both can make them on the sides. Since more points are scored with shots down the side walls, the latter positioning is the preferred one. With the players' forehands to the side, the middle is the weak spot; let the player with the stronger backhand take the middle shots. Usually this will occur near the front court, since a player can often "run around" a shot that is hit into the back, and take it with his forehand.

Front and back method   In this method, the one player stands in front (in a mid-court position near the short line), and his partner stands behind him (in the middle of the back court area). The front player handles all short shots, and the partner takes all shots traveling into the back court.

For intermediate and advanced players, this is not as desirable a court coverage system as the side by side: There is a lack of protection against shots which come down the

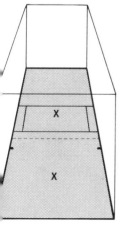

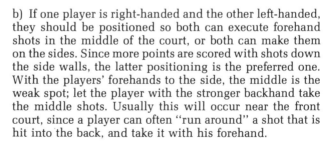

at and back method of doubles
rt coverage

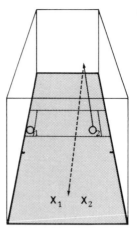

← Doubles serve strategy: Opponent O₂ hits a low drive serve down the center of the court to players X₁ and X₂'s backhands (player X₁ is left-handed)

sides of the court—where most points are scored. It quires a very quick player in the front, and a good shoo and ceiling ball player in the back. This is usually too mu work for the back court player and too much responsibil for the front court partner. Beginners, however, are co fortable with this formation, since it requires less tea work than the side by side method. Each player's sponsibility for coverage is well defined. If one of teammates is a much weaker player, or is less "in sha than the other, he is usually placed in the front positic where he will not have to work as hard.

Shot selection

In doubles, the strategic value of a particular shot var according to the effectiveness of the opponent's co coverage. Since *any* team is *potentially* capable of ext sive court coverage and a strong defense, defensive sh should be emphasized and offensive shots used discri inately. A team should try to keep the ball in play u a good opportunity for an offensive shot arises—m likely in the front part of the court.

Serve strategy

The doubles serve is less of an offensive shot than in s gles, but nevertheless a good server will try to limit possibilities of an opponent's offensive return. In orc to make the most of his serves, the doubles player shou

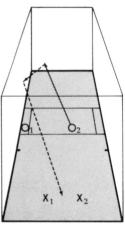

Doubles serve strategy: Opponent O₂ hits a low cross-court serve to the center of the court (to the backhands of players X₁ and X₂)

a) Experiment with various types of serves—to be opponents and to different spots on the court, te ing for weaknesses.

b) Serve to the weaker player's weakest side. If a we spot is found, continue exploiting it.

c) Try a low drive serve down the center of the co or a low cross-court serve angling into the cent when the opponents are stationed with their fo hands toward the side walls (which a right- a left-handed opposing team might do).

d) Make sure all lob serves are hit properly—high a deep, brushing the side wall—otherwise an opp nent may cut off the shot. On garbage serves, low the altitude to prevent a volley return.

If the right-side player is serving, his partner should s tion himself in the left side of the service box, and v versa. A player cannot leave the service box until partner has served and the ball has passed the short li If the server hits his partner while he is in the service b the ball is ruled dead, and replayed. After the ball is serv it is most important that both partners move to their pro positions—behind the short line and away from the si walls—to await the opponent's return.

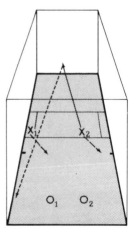

Doubles serve strategy: After the serve, both players X₁ and X₂ must move to their proper court coverage positions (side-by-side coverage)

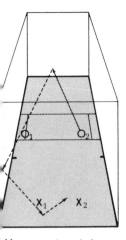

bles serve return strategy:
pponent O₂ serves a hard
ve which hits the side wall
ve waist height and angles
e into the back wall, player
nay be in the best position to
a return

Serve return strategy

The most reliable strategy on serve returns is to let the partner who has the best shot at the ball do the returning. For example, if the serve hits the left side wall and rebounds across the court and into the backwall, the partner on the right side may be in the best position for making the play.

The player who returns the serve should try to direct the ball toward the weaker opponent's weakest side. This is not always possible, but it should be kept in mind. In general, defensive serve returns are the best. The most effective are the ceiling, around-the-wall, and Z shots. An attempt should be made to volley all high serves (garbage, Z, lob) before the ball has a chance to reach the floor. This is easily accomplished in doubles, since each serve returner has to cover only one half of the receiving area.

Rally strategy

During a doubles rally you should generally:

a) Exploit your opponents' weaknesses.

b) Move into good court position while your partner is hitting the ball.

c) Hit a defensive shot (ceiling, Z, lob, around-the-wall ball) to the back court if your partner is out of position. This will allow him time to regain his position.

d) Hit all Z or around-the-wall shots in a manner so your opponent cannot cut them off before they reach the back court.

e) Hit all ceiling balls and pass shots soft enough so the ball does not rebound hard off the back wall, making an easy setup.

For the most part, rally shots in doubles must be hit more accurately, and harder, than in singles. Pass shots are not nearly as effective as in the singles game.

Offensive shots are best used when one, or both, members of the opposing team are caught out of position or have hit a weak service return. In most cases a pinch shot, directed away from the closest opponent, is the best kill to use, but a front wall-side wall kill is also effective. In general, hit hard offensive shots, either kills or passes, since they cause hurried, inaccurate responses, especially among beginners. A wide-angle V pass is extremely effective if both opponents happen to be in the front court, or if they are a right- and left-handed combination. This shot tends to jam the opponents. A drive that is directed down the middle of the court, toward the backhands of a right- and left-handed team will also work well.

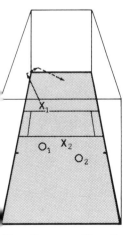

bles rally strategy: Player X₁
n front court and opponent
s out of position on the op-
ite side of the court. Player
ises a pinch shot which
vels away from his closest
onent, O₂

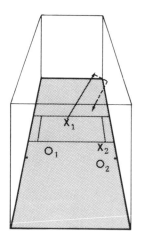 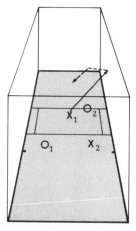 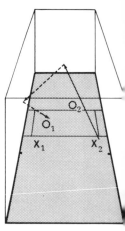

Doubles rally strategy: player X_1 is in mid court and opponent O_2 is out of position (deep). Player X_1 hits a front wall-side wall kill which travels into O_2's open area

Doubles rally strategy: Player X_1 is in mid court and opponent O_2 is out of position in the front court. Player X_1 hits a pinch shot away from opponent O_2

Doubles rally strategy: Both o ponents O_1 and O_2 are in or ne front court. Player X_2 hits a w angle V-pass which jams oppe ent O_1

Isolation is a strategic ploy used during rallies to kee particular opposing team member from hitting too ma shots. There are three main types:

a) *Strong player isolation.* The object here is for a te to hit every shot to the opposing team's wea player.

b) *Forehand player isolation.* If the opposing te members are both right-handed or both left-hand all shots are directed to the opponent whose ba hand is toward a side wall. Against two right-hand all shots are placed along the left side wall, and v versa against two left-handers.

c) *"Hot" player isolation.* In the case when one p ticular opponent is hitting the ball especially w a good doubles team will attempt to "cool him c by hitting everything to his partner.

As a player becomes more seriously involved in racquetball, he may entertain the thought of entering a tournament. If he does so, he will usually be asked by the tournament officials to referee a match. The racquetball referee is the sole official of the game; he not only calls and keeps the score, but also acts as arbitrator, interpreter, and enforcer. The best referees are invisible during a match. When their voices are heard, they make their calls with authority.

PRE-MATCH DUTIES

A good referee is organized and well prepared. Nothi
should be left to chance:

1 The court should be examined for possible *court h*
 ders. These are obstructions on the court that cat
 the ball to bounce irregularly. The referee must be a
 to recognize these untrue bounces during a match, a
 make the appropriate call. Good examples of co
 hinders are lights which are not perfectly flush w
 the ceiling, and doors which are not flush with 1
 wall. An upstairs gallery is also considered a co
 hinder in the situation where a ball goes into it a
 hitting the front wall.

2 Towels are needed for the players and for the floor i
 becomes wet.

3 A minimum of two game balls must be on hand. T
 players should be allowed to hit the balls while tl
 are warming up. After deciding which will be the ga
 ball, the players must hand the second ball to the 1
 eree. This ball is kept as a replacement in case the fi
 ball breaks.

4 The two linesmen should be positioned so their va
 tage points are as different from the referee's, and fr
 each other's, as possible. Their placement deper
 upon the type of court:

 a. On courts that have no glass walls and only balco
 viewing, the referee should be equidistant from 1
 side walls, a linesman at his right and left, abc
 the rear corners:

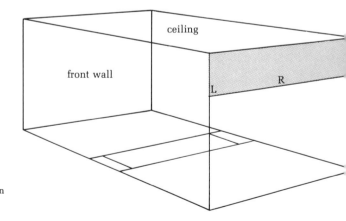

R = referee
L = linesman

Balcony on back wall, no glass
side walls

b. On courts where only the back wall is glass, again the referee is in the center, with linesmen at the corners:

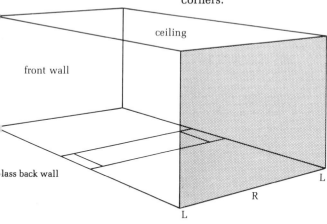

c. On courts with glass side walls, the referee is centered behind the back wall if it is glass, or upstairs if there is only a balcony. The linesmen are positioned at, or just behind, the short line on opposite sides of the court:

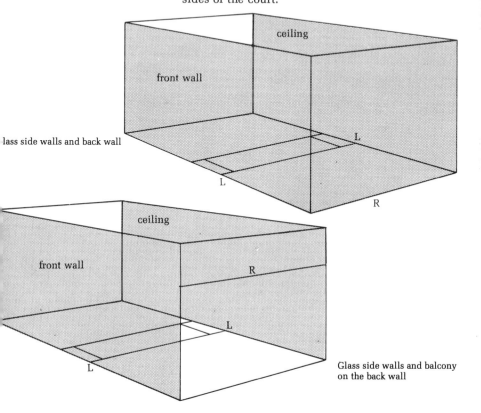

Glass side walls and balcony on the back wall

d. On courts that have only one glass side wall, the referee is located at the middle of the back wall with one linesman at the short line and the other along the glass side wall at the referee's level:

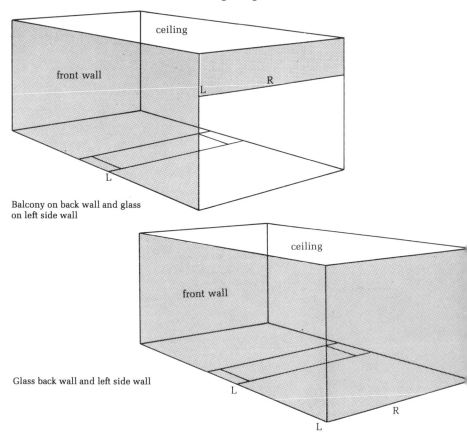

Balcony on back wall and glass on left side wall

Glass back wall and left side wall

5 The referee should introduce the linesmen to the players and discuss their roles:

a. They may not initiate a call, but only give an opinion if the referee cannot make a call or the call is appealed.

b. The linesmen are not to talk. If asked for an opinion on a call, they are to signal "thumbs up" if they agree with the referee and "thumbs down" if they disagree. If a linesman does not see the play, or cannot make a decision, he must signal with his hand palm down, making a back and forth gesture.

c. In order to reverse a ruling, both linesmen must disagree with the referee. If the referee makes a call and one linesman disagrees while the other declines to make a call, the referee's decision stands.

6 Court hinders, hinders, avoidable hinders, technical fouls, the ten-second rule, and appeals are discussed. The referee should inform the players of the rules and their interpretations:

   a. The players are requested to call their own skip balls and double bounce pickups.

   b. The server must not serve until the score is announced. Once the score is called, the players have ten seconds in which to either serve or get ready to receive.

   c. The only hinder a player may call is contact with the opposition on the backswing. This is an automatic hinder, but it must be called immediately or else the shot will stand.

   d. Avoidable hinders will be called without prior warnings. Technical fouls which result in a point loss for the offender will be called, but warnings may be issued first.

   e. Players are allowed to question a call if the referee misses it—only if they do so calmly and respectfully.

CALLING THE MATCH

It is very important that the referee strive to maintain consistency in his calls. They should be made loud and clear. Decisiveness is essential. When calling the score, the referee should make uniform, well timed calls. Since the announcement of the score is the signal to begin play, the referee should wait until both players are almost ready. The server is usually the first to get set, so the referee should begin to announce the score just as the receiver is preparing himself. The score should be called immediately if the receiver is ready first. During a match the referee will have to stop play from time to time. If the stoppage is not for a hinder, the referee should call, "Hold it!" or "Stop play!" If a hinder occurs, the referee should call, "Hinder!"

A referee may have to make several difficult decisions during a game. Being able to call them correctly, without variance, requires a thorough knowledge of the rules. Some of the more important ones follow:

1 *Appealable calls.* There are only six specific situations in which a player can appeal a call by the referee. Hinders, avoidable hinders, and technicals cannot be appealed. The appealable situations are:

   a. A "skip" call by the referee on a ball the player thinks is good.

   b. "No call" on a ball the player thinks skipped into the front wall.

c. A "short" call on a serve the player thinks is goo

d. "No call" on a serve the player thinks is short.

e. A "two bounce" call on a shot the player believ
   he reached in one bounce.

f. "No call" on a shot the player thinks his oppone
   picked up in two bounces.

Appeals must be made directly to the referee. The refere
then checks his linesmen for their opinion.

2 *Skip balls.* Ball sound and spin are the two indicato
which help the referee tell whether or not the ba
skipped into the front wall. A "squeaking" sound (ru
ber sliding on wood) and an increase in backspin as tl
ball rebounds off the wall indicate a skip ball. A sh
which is good makes a solid "thunk" sound, and usual
carries topspin after contacting the front wall.

3 *Hinders.* A *hinder* is any unintentional interferen
by a player which prevents an opponent from havi
a fair chance to see or return the ball. Examples includ

a. Any object or irregular part of the court which
   struck by the ball, and causes an erratic bounce.

b. Any unintentional bodily contact with anoth
   player which interferes with his vision, or retu
   of the ball.

c. A ball which hits the opponent on the fly befo
   reaching the front wall.

d. A ball which passes too close to the body of t.
   player who just hit it, thus preventing the opposi
   player from seeing it.

e. A ball which returns through the legs of the play
   who just hit it (not an automatic call).

Hinder judgments are entirely the referee's respon
bility; players' opinions should not be sought. If a play
believes there is any danger of hitting the oppone
with racquet or ball, he must hold up his swing. In tl
case the referee must give him the benefit of the dot
and call a safety hinder unless there is obviously
risk of injury. In all cases of hinders the rally is replaye
The referee cannot allow a player to hit the ball, a
then give him the choice of accepting the shot or t
hinder. If the shot is taken, there is no hinder. Al:
if a player's sight, or path to the ball, is blocked but t
referee decides that he could not reach the shot ev
in normal circumstances, then a hinder is not called

4 *Avoidable hinders.* There are four specific situatio
in which an offense can be described as an *avoidal*
hinder. Each offense leads to a point, or handout, agaiı
the committing party. An avoidable hinder is not nec
sarily a *deliberate* one, though in certain cases it is.

a. *Failure to move.* This hinder occurs when one play
   does not move sufficiently to allow his oppone

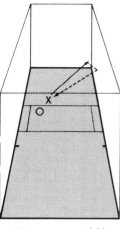

Player X creates an avoidable hinder by not moving out of the way of player O after taking his shot

his shot. A player must get out of the way of an opponent, even if it will result in loss of the rally. Not moving because of fear of collision, or because of ignorance of the opponent's location, cannot be excused. It is the obligation of a player to look over his shoulder, and, if necessary, get out of the way. If a player hinders the opponent's shot in any way, an avoidable hinder should be called.

b. *Blocking.* This occurs when one player moves into a position effecting a block on the opponent about to return the ball, or in doubles, when one partner moves in front of an opponent as his partner is returning the ball. In the first case, which applies mainly to singles, the blocker usually realizes that he is making an illegal block. If he hits a poor shot, for example, which allows his opponent an easy setup, he may move in on him and try to claim a safety hinder, while he is actually obstructing his opponent. This usually occurs from behind, and often results in the blocker getting hit by his opponent's racquet because he is too close.

Player X creates an avoidable hinder by hitting a setup to player O and then moving so close to player O that he interferes with his stroke

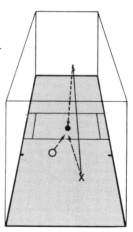

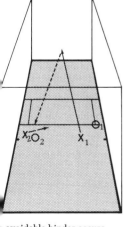

An avoidable hinder occurs when the right side player from team X hits a cross-court pass and his teammate moves in front of the left side opponent, thereby blocking his view

The blocking situation which relates to doubles play is one of the most difficult avoidable hinders to detect. It occurs, for example, when a player on the right side of the court hits a cross-court pass and at the same moment his partner moves directly in front of his opponent on the left side. The shot will probably never be seen by the opponent who is being blocked, and will lead, at best, to a weak return. This, too, is an avoidable hinder.

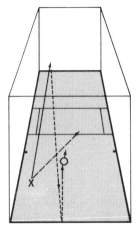

Player X commits an avoidable hinder as he moves into the path of the ball hit by player O

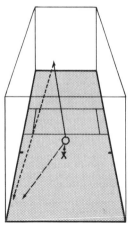

An avoidable hinder is committed when player X pushes player O as he retreats for the ball

c. *Hit by the ball.* In this instance, a player moves in the way, and is struck by the ball just played by his opponent. This may occur almost anywhere on the court, but usually takes place when the ball rebounds off the back wall, giving a player time to move into blocking position. This maneuver is an obvious attempt to prohibit an opponent's shot from following its natural course, and is easy to detect.

d. *Deliberate pushing.* This occurs when a player deliberately pushes or shoves an opponent during volley. Pushing is an avoidable hinder because:

- It gives the player who is pushing off an unfair start when retrieving the shot.
- It often causes the player being pushed to lose his balance, putting him in an awkward position to retrieve the next shot.
- Injury may result.

A prospective offender is the player who rushes in to cover an opponent's shot. If the opponent sees this move, and then hits a ceiling or pass shot, the player may push off the opponent as he changes direction to make his retrieve.

Two other specific examples of avoidable hinders need to be mentioned. The first occurs when a player dives for a shot, returns the ball, and in regaining his feet blocks his opponent, moves into the path of the ball or fails to move as the ball rebounds toward him. The diving player has every right to regain his feet, but he must let his opponent have his shot. The second example occurs when a player yells or stamps his feet as his opponent is about to hit a shot. This is an avoidable hinder, and can also be punishable as unsportsmanlike conduct.

5 *Technicals.* U.S.R.A. and N.R.C. rules state that:

The referee is empowered, after giving due warning, to deduct one point from a contestant's or his team's total score when in the referee's sole judgment, the contestant during the course of the match is being overtly and deliberately abusive beyond a point of reason. The warning referred to will be called a *Technical Warning* and the actual invoking of the penalty is called a *Referee's Technical.* If after the technical is called against the abusing contestant and the play is not immediately continued within the allotted time provided for under the existing rules, the referee is empowered to forfeit the match in favor of the abusing contestant's opponent or opponents as the case may be. The Referee's Technical can be invoked by the referee as many times during the course of a match as he deems necessary.

Explanations to several of the references in the technical foul rule follow:

a. "After due warning." The warning is given when the referee instructs the players prior to a match that he will call a referee's technical if conditions warrant it. However, additional warnings may be given during a match if the referee thinks the situation requires more discretion.

b. Point deduction from the offender's score. This insures that no match or game can be won or lost on a technical foul. The winner must earn his victory and not get it on a judgment ruling. The serving order of the game is not disturbed, only the score.

c. "In the sole judgment of the referee." Only a referee can invoke the technical foul rule—not a linesman, club owner, or tournament director.

d. "Beyond the point of reason." Several examples are: profanity, obscene gestures, any argument extending beyond the ten-second service period, leaving the court without permission, and excessive striking of the ball after play has ended (especially after a warning has been given).

The referee must always remember that a player has the right to question a call if he believes a mistake in ruling has been made. Discretion should be used by the referee in this instance, and play should be resumed as soon as possible.

6 *Forfeiting a match.* Forfeiture may occur if a player:

a. Is injured and he cannot resume play.

b. Is not present at the start of the match.

c. Resorts to physical violence.

d. Continues conducting himself in an unsportsmanlike manner after two technical fouls have been called on him.

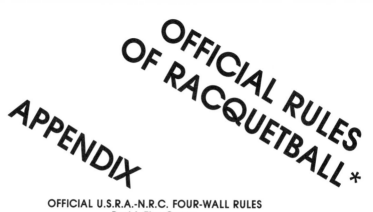

OFFICIAL U.S.R.A.-N.R.C. FOUR-WALL RULES
Part I. The Game

Rule 1.1   Types of games. Racquetball may be played by two or four players. When played by two it is called "singles"; and when played by four, "doubles."

Rule 1.2   Description. Racquetball, as the name implies, is a competitive game in which a racquet is used to serve and return the ball.

Rule 1.3   Objective. The objective is to win each volley by serving or returning the ball so the opponent is unable to keep the ball in play. A serve or volley is won when a side is unable to return the ball before it touches the floor twice.

Rule 1.4   Points and outs. Points are scored only by the serving side when it serves an ace or wins a volley. When the serving side loses a volley it loses the serve. Losing the serve is called a "hand-out."

Rule 1.5   Game. A game is won by the side first scoring 21 points.

Rule 1.6   Match. A match is won by the side first winning two games.

Part II. Court and Equipment

Rule 2.1   Court. The specifications for the standard four-wall racquetball court are:

    (a) **Dimension.** The dimensions shall be 20 feet wide, 20 feet high, and 40 feet long, with back wall at least 12 feet high.

    (b) **Lines and zones.** Racquetball courts shall be divided and marked on the floors with 1½ inch wide red or white lines as follows:

        (1) **Short line.** The short line is midway between and is parallel with the front and back walls dividing the court into equal front and back courts.

        (2) **Service line.** The service line is parallel with and located 5 feet in front of the short line.

        (3) **Service zone.** The service zone is the space between the outer edges of the short and service lines.

        (4) **Service boxes.** A service box is located at each end of the service zone by lines 18 inches from and parallel with each side wall.

        (5) **Receiving lines.** Five feet back of the short line, vertical lines shall be marked on each side wall extending 3 inches from the floor. See rule 4.7(a).

Rule 2.2   Ball specifications. The specifications for the standard racquetball are:

    (a) **Official Ball.** The official ball of the U.S.R.A. is the black Seamco 558; the official ball of the N.R.C. is the green Seamco 559; or any other racquetball deemed official by the U.S.R.A. or N.R.C. from time to time. The ball shall be 2¼ inches in diameter; weight approximately 1.40 ounces with the bounce at 68-72 inches from 100 inch drop at a temperature of 76 degrees F.

Rule 2.3   Ball selection. A new ball shall be selected by the referee for use in each match in all tournaments. During a game the referee may, at his discretion or at the request of both players or teams, select another ball. Balls that are not round or which bounce erratically shall not be used.

Rule 2.4   Racquet. The official racquet will have a maximum head length of 11 inches and a width of 9 inches. These measurements are computed from the outer edge of the

*Published by The United States Racquetball Association and National Racquetball Club. Reprinted by permission.

racquet head rims. The handle may not exceed 7 inches in length. Total length and wi‹ of the racquet may not exceed a total of 27 inches.

    (a) The racquet must include a thong which must be securely wrapped on the play‹ wrist.

    (b) The racquet frame may be made of any material, as long as it conforms to the ab‹ specifications.

    (c) The strings of the racquet may be gut, monofilament, nylon or metal.

Rule 2.5   Uniform. All parts of the uniform, consisting of shirt, shorts and socks, sł be clean, white or of bright colors. Warmup pants and shirts, if worn in actual match pl shall also be white or of bright colors, but may be of any color if not used in match pl Only club insignia, name of club, name of racquetball organization, name of tourname or name of sponsor may be on the uniform. Players may not play without shirts.

Part III. Officiating

Rule 3.1   Tournaments. All tournaments shall be managed by a committee or chairm‹ who shall designate the officials.

Rule 3.2   Officials. The officials shall include a referee and a scorer. Additional assist‹ and record keepers may be designated as desired.

Rule 3.3   Qualifications. Since the quality of the officiating often determines the succ of each tournament, all officials shall be experienced or trained, and shall be thoroug familiar with these rules and with the local playing conditions.

Rule 3.4   Rule briefing. Before all tournaments, all officials and players shall be brie on rules and on local court hinders or other regulations.

Rule 3.5   Referees. (a) Pre-match duties. Before each match commences, it shall be duty of the referee to:

    (1) Check on adequacy of preparation of the court with respect to cleanlin‹ lighting and temperature, and upon location of locker rooms, drinking fo‹ tains, etc.

    (2) Check on availability and suitability of all materials necessary for the ma‹ such as balls, towels, score cards and pencils.

    (3) Check readiness and qualifications of assisting officials.

    (4) Explain court regulations to players and inspect the compliance of racqu with rules.

    (5) Remind players to have an adequate supply of extra racquets and uniform

    (6) Introduce players, toss coin, and signal start of first game.

  (b) Decisions. During games the referee shall decide all questions that may arise accordance with these rules. If there is body contact on the back swing, the pla should call it quickly. This is the only call a player may make. On all questi‹ involving judgment and on all questions not covered by these rules, the decis of the referee is final.

  (c) Protests. Any decision not involving the judgment of the referee may on pro‹ be decided by the chairman, if present, or his delegated representative.

  (d) Forefeitures. A match may be forfeited by the referee when:

    (1) Any player refuses to abide by the referee's decision, or engages in unspo‹ manlike conduct.

    (2) After warning any player leaves the court without permission of the refe during a game.

    (3) Any player for a singles match, or any team for a doubles match fails to re‹ to play. Normally, 20 minutes from the scheduled game time will be allo‹ before forfeiture. The tournament chairman may permit a longer delay if cumstances warrant such a decision.

    (4) If both players for a singles, or both teams for doubles fail to appear to ‹ for consolation matches or other play-offs, they shall forfeit their ratings future tournaments, and forfeit any trophies, medals, awards, or prize mon

Rule 3.5 (e) Referee's technical. The referee is empowered, after giving due warning, to deduct one point from a contestant's or his team's total score when in the referee's sole judgment, the contestant during the course of the match is being overtly and deliberately abusive beyond a point of reason. The warning referred to will be called a "**Technical warning**" and the actual invoking of this penalty is called a "**Referee's technical.**" If after the technical is called against the abusing contestant and the play is not immediately continued within the allotted time provided for under the existing rules, the referee is empowered to forfeit the match in favor of the abusing contestant's opponent or opponents as the case may be. The "**Referee's technical**" can be invoked by the referee as many times during the course of a match as he deems necessary.

Rule 3.6 Scorers. The scorer shall keep a record of the progress of the game in the manner prescribed by the committee or chairman. As a minimum the progress record shall include the order of serves, outs, and points. The referee or scorer shall announce the score before each serve.

Rule 3.7 Record keepers. In addition to the scorer, the committee may designate additional persons to keep more detailed records for statistical purposes of the progress of the game.

Rule 3.8 Linesmen. In any U.S.R.A. or N.R.C. sanctioned tournament match, linesmen may be designated in order to help decide appealed rulings. Two linesmen will be designated by the tournament chairman, and shall, at the referee's signal either agree or disagree with the referee's ruling.

The official signal by a linesman to show agreement with the referee is "thumbs up." The official signal to show disagreement is "thumbs down." The official signal for no opinion is an "open palm down."

Both linesmen must disagree with the referee in order to reverse his ruling. If one linesman agrees and one linesman disagrees or has no opinion the referee's call shall stand.

Rule 3.9 Appeals. In any U.S.RA. or N.R.C. sanctioned tournament match using linesmen, a player or team may appeal certain calls by the referee. These calls are 1) kill shots (whether good or bad); 2) short serves; and 3) double bounce pick ups. At no time may a player or team appeal hinder, avoidable hinder or technical foul calls.

The appeal must be directed to the referee, who will then request opinions from the linesmen. Any appeal made directly to a linesman by a player or team will be considered null and void, and forfeit any appeal rights for that player or team for that particular rally.

(a) **Kill shot appeals.** If the referee makes a call of "good" on a kill shot attempt which ends a particular rally, the loser of the rally may appeal the call, if he feels the shot was not good. If the appeal is successful and the referee's original call reversed, the player who originally lost the rally is declared winner of the rally and is entitled to every benefit under the rules as such, i.e., point and/or service.

If the referee makes a call of "bad" or "skip" on a kill shot attempt, he has ended the rally. The player against whom the call went has the right to appeal the call, if he feels the shot was good. If the appeal is successful and the referee's original call reversed, the player who originally lost the rally is declared winner of the rally and is entitled to every benefit under the rules as winner of a rally.

(b) **Short serve appeals.** If the referee makes a call of "short" on a serve that the server felt was good, the server may appeal the call. If his appeal is successful, the server is then entitled to two additional serves.

If the served ball was considered by the referee to be an ACE serve to the crotch of the floor and side wall and in his opinion there was absolutely no way for the receiver to return the serve, then a point shall be awarded to the server.

If the referee makes a "no call" on a particular serve (therefore making it a legal serve) but either player feels the serve was short, either player may appeal the call at the end of the rally. If the loser of the rally appeals and wins his appeal, then the situation reverts back to the point of service with the call becoming "short." If it was a first service, one more serve attempt is allowed. If the server already had one fault, this second fault would cause a side out.

(c) **Double bounce pick-up appeals.** If the referee makes a call of "two bounces thereby stopping play, the player against whom the call was made has the rig of appeal, if he feels he retrieved the ball legally. If the appeal is upheld, the ral is re-played.

If the referee makes no call on a particular play during the course of a rally in whi one player feels his opponent retrieved a ball on two or more bounces, the play feeling this way has the right of appeal. However, since the ball is in play, tl player wishing to appeal must clearly motion to the referee and linesmen, therel alerting them to the exact play which is being appealed. At the same time, tl player appealing must continue to retrieve and play the rally.

If the appealing player should win the rally, no appeal is necessary. If he loses tl rally, and his appeal is upheld, the call is reversed and the "good" retrieve l his opponent becomes a "double bounce pick-up," making the appealing play the winner of the rally and entitled to all benefits thereof.

Rule 3.10 If at any time during the course of a match the referee is of the opinion th a player or team is deliberately abusing the right of appeal, by either repetitious appea of obvious rulings, or as a means of unsportsmanlike conduct, the referee shall enfor the Technical Foul rule.

Part IV. Play Regulations

Rule 4.1   Serve-Generally. (a) Order. The player or side winning the toss becomes tl first server and starts the first game, and the third game, if any.

(b) **Start.** Games are started from any place in the service zone. No part of either fo may extend beyond either line of the service zone. Stepping on the line (but n beyond it) is permitted. Server must remain in the service zone until the serv ball passes short line. Violations are called "foot faults."

(d) **Manner.** A serve is commenced by bouncing the ball to the floor in the servi zone, and on the first bounce the ball is struck by the server's racquet so that hits the front wall and on the rebound hits the floor back of the short line, eith with or without touching one of the side walls.

(e) **Readiness.** Serves shall not be made until the receiving side is ready, or the refer has called play ball.

Rule 4.2   Serve-in doubles. (a) Server. At the beginning of each game in doubles, ea side shall inform the referee of the order of service, which order shall be followed throug out the game. Only the first server serves the first time up and continues to serve fi throughout the game. When the first server is out—the side is out. Thereafter both playe on each side shall serve until a hand-out occurs. It is not necessary for the server to i ternate serves to their opponents.

(b) **Partner's position.** On each serve, the server's partner shall stand erect with I back to the side wall and with both feet on the floor within the service box un the served ball passes the short line. Violations are called "foot faults."

Rule 4.3   Defective serves. Defective serves are of three types resulting in penalties follows:

(a) **Dead ball serve.** A dead ball serve results in no penalty and the server is giv another serve without cancelling a prior illegal serve.

(b) **Fault serve.** Two fault serves results in a hand-out.

(c) **Out serves.** An out serve results in a hand-out.

Rule 4.4   Dead ball serves. Dead ball serves do not cancel any previous illegal ser They occur when an otherwise legal serve:

(a) **Hits partner.** Hits the server's partner on the fly on the rebound from the fro wall while the server's partner is in the service box. Any serve that touches t floor before hitting the partner in the box is a short.

(b) **Screen balls.** Passes too close to the server or the server's partner to obstruct t view of the returning side. Any serve passing behind the server's partner and t side wall is an automatic screen.

(c) **Court hinders.** Hits any part of the court that under local rules is a dead ball.

Rule 4.5 Fault serves. The following serves are faults and any two in succession results in a handout:

    (a) Foot faults. A foot faults results:

        (1) When the server leaves the service zone before the served ball passes the short line.

        (2) When the server's partner leaves the service box before the served ball passes the short line.

    (b) Short serve. A short serve is any served ball that first hits the front wall and on the rebound hits the floor in front of the back edge of the short line either with or without touching one side wall.

    (c) Two-side serve. A two-side serve is any ball served that first hits the front wall and on the rebound hits two side walls on the fly.

    (d) Ceiling serve. A ceiling serve is any served ball that touches the ceiling after hitting the front wall either with or without touching one side wall.

    (e) Long serve. A long serve is any served ball that first hits the front wall and rebounds to the back wall before touching the floor.

    (f) Out of court serve. Any ball going out of the court on the serve.

Rule 4.6 Out serves. Any one of the following serves results in a hand-out:

    (a) Bounces. Bouncing the ball more than three times while in the service zone before striking the ball. A bounce is a drop or throw to the floor, followed by a catch. The ball may not be bounced anywhere but on the floor within the serve zone. Accidental dropping of the ball counts as one bounce.

    (b) Missed ball. Any attempt to strike the ball on the first bounce that results either in a total miss or in touching any part of the server's body other than his racquet.

    (c) Non-front serve. Any served ball that strikes the server's partner, or the ceiling, floor or side wall, before striking the front wall.

    (d) Touched serve. Any served ball that on the rebound from the front wall touches the server, or touches the server's partner while any part of his body is out of the service box, or the server's partner intentionally catches the served ball on the fly.

    (e) Out-of-order serve. In doubles, when either partner serves out of order.

    (f) Crotch serve. If the served ball hits the crotch in the front wall it is considered the same as hitting the floor and is an out. A crotch serve into the back wall is good and in play.

Rule 4.7 Return of serve. (a) Receiving Position. The receiver or receivers must stand at least 5 feet back of the short line, as indicated by the 3 inch vertical line on each side wall, and cannot return the ball until it passes the short line. Any infraction results in a point for the server.

    (b) Defective serve. To eliminate any misunderstanding, the receiving side should not catch or touch a defectively served ball until called by the referee or it has touched the floor the second time.

    (c) Fly return. In making a fly return the receiver must end up with both feet back of the service zone. A violation by a receiver results in a point for the server.

    (d) Legal return. After the ball is legally served, one of the players on the receiving side must strike the ball with his racquet either on the fly or after the first bounce and before the ball touches the floor the second time to return the ball to the front wall either directly or after touching one or both side walls, the back wall or the ceiling, or any combination of those surfaces. A returned ball may not touch the floor before touching the front wall. (1) It is legal to return the ball by striking the ball into the back wall first, then hitting the front wall on the fly or after hitting the side wall or ceiling.

    (e) Failure to return. The failure to return a serve results in a point for the server.

Rule 4.8 Changes of serve. (a) Hand-out. A server is entitled to continue serving until:

        (1) **Out serve.** He makes an out serve under Rule 4.6 or

        (2) **Fault serves.** He makes two fault serves in succession under Rule 4.5, or

(3) **Hits partner.** He hits his partner with an attempted return before the ba touches the floor the second time, or

(4) **Return failure.** He or his partner fails to keep the ball in play by returning as required by Rule 4.7(d), or

(5) **Avoidable hinder.** He or his partner commits an avoidable hinder unde Rule 4.11.

(b) **Side-out** (1) **In singles.** In singles, retiring the server retires the side.

(2) **In doubles.** In doubles, the side is retired when both partners have been p out, except on the first serve as provided in Rule 4.2 (a).

(c) **Effect.** When the server on the side loses the serve, the server or serving side sha become the receiver; and the receiving side, the server; and so alternately in a subsequent services of the game:

Rule 4.9 Volleys. Each legal return after the serve is called a volley. Play during volley shall be according to the following rules:

(a) **One or both hands.** Only the head of the racquet may be used at any time to retur the ball. The ball must be hit with the racquet in one or both hands. Switchin hands to hit a ball is out. The use of any portion of the body is an out.

(b) **One touch.** In attempting returns, the ball may be touched only once by one play on returning side. In doubles both partners may swing at, but only one, may h the ball. Each violation of (a) or (b) results in a hand-out or point.

(c) **Return attempts.** (1) **In singles.** In singles if a player swings at but misses the ba in play, the player may repeat his attempts to return the ball until it touches th floor the second time.

(2) **In doubles.** In doubles if one player swings at but misses the ball, both he an his partner may make further attempts to return the ball until it touches th floor the second time. Both partners on a side are entitled to an attempt return the ball.

(3) **Hinders.** In singles or doubles, if a player swings at but misses the ball in pla and in his, or his partner's attempt again to play the ball there is an unintel tional interference by an opponent it shall be a hinder. (See Rule 4.10).

(d) **Touching ball.** Except as provided in Rule 4.10(a) (2), any touching of a ball b fore it touches the floor the second time by a player other than the one making return is a point or out against the offending player.

(e) **Out of court ball.** (1) **After return.** Any ball returned to the front wall which on th rebound or on the first bounce goes into the gallery or through any opening i a side wall shall be declared dead and the serve replayed.

(2) **No return.** Any ball not returned to the front wall, but which caroms off player's racquet into the gallery or into any opening in a side wall either wii or without touching the ceiling, side or back wall, shall be an out or poil against the players failing to make the return.

(f) **Dry ball.** During the game and particularly on service every effort should be mai to keep the ball dry. Deliberately wetting shall result in an out. The ball may l inspected by the referee at any time during a game.

(g) **Broken ball.** If there is any suspicion that a ball has broken on the serve or durii a volley, play shall continue until the end of the volley. The referee or any play may request the ball be examined. If the referee decides the ball is broken or othe wise defective, a new ball shall be put into play and the point replayed.

(h) **Play stoppage.** (1) If a player loses a shoe or other equipment, or foreign objec enter the court, or any other outside interference occurs, the referee shall st the play. (2) If a player loses control of his racquet, time should be called after tl point has been decided, providing the racquet does not strike an opponent or ii terfere with ensuing play.

Rule 4.10 Dead ball hinders. Hinders are of two types—"dead ball" and "avoidable Dead ball hinders as described in this rule result in the point being replayed. Avoidab hinders are described in Rule 4.11.

(a) **Situations.** When called by the referee, the following are dead ball hinders:

(1) **Court hinders.** Hits any part of the court which under local rules is a dead ball.

(2) **Hitting opponent.** Any returned ball that touches an opponent on the fly before it returns to the front wall.

(3) **Body contact.** Any body contact with an opponent that interferes with seeing or returning the ball.

(4) **Screen ball.** Any ball rebounding from the front wall close to the body of a player on the side which just returned the ball, to interfere with or prevent the returning side from seeing the ball. See Rule 4.4 (b).

(5) **Straddle ball.** A ball passing between the legs of a player on the side which just returned the ball, if there is no fair chance to see or return the ball.

(6) **Other interference.** Any other unintentional inteference which prevents an opponent from having a fair chance to see or return the ball.

(b) **Effect.** A call by the referee of a "hinder" stops the play and voids any situation following, such as the ball hitting a player. No player is authorized to call a hinder, except on the back swing and such a call must be made immediately as provided in Rule 3.5 (b).

(c) **Avoidance.** While making an attempt to return the ball, a player is entitled to a fair chance to see and return the ball. It is the duty of the side that has just served or returned the ball to move so that the receiving side may go straight to the ball and not be required to go around an opponent. The referee should be liberal in calling hinders to discourage any practice of playing the ball where an adversary cannot see it until too late. It is no excuse that the ball is "killed," unless in the opinion of the referee he couldn't return the ball. Hinders should be called without a claim by a player, especially in close plays and on game points.

(d) **In doubles.** In doubles, both players on a side are entitled to a fair and unobstructed chance at the ball and either one is entitled to a hinder even though it naturally would be his partner's ball and even though his partner may have attempted to play the ball or that he may already have missed it. It is not a hinder when one player hinders his partner.

Rule 4.11   Avoidable hinders. An avoidable hinder results in an "out" or a point depending upon whether the offender was serving or receiving.

(a) **Failure to move.** Does not move sufficiently to allow opponent his shot.

(b) **Blocking.** Moves into a position effecting a block, on the opponent about to return the ball, or, in doubles, one partner moves in front of an opponent as his partner is returning the ball.

(c) **Moving into ball.** Moves in the way and is struck by the ball just played by his opponent.

(d) **Pushing.** Deliberately pushing or shoving an opponent during a volley.

Rule 4.12   Rest periods. (a) Delays. Deliberate delay exceeding ten seconds by server, or receiver shall result in an out or point against the offender.

(b) **During game.** During a game each player in singles, or each side in doubles, either while serving or receiving may request a "time out" for a towel, wiping glasses, change or adjustment. Each "time out" shall not exceed 30 seconds. No more than three "time outs" in a game shall be granted each singles player or each team in doubles.

(c) **Injury.** No time out shall be charged to a player who is injured during play. An injured player shall not be allowed more than a total of fifteen minutes of rest. If the injured player is not able to resume play after total rests of 15 minutes the match shall be awarded to the opponent or opponents. On any further injury to same player, the Commissioner, if present, or committee, after considering any available medical opinion shall determine whether the injured player will be allowed to continue.

(d) **Between games.** A five minute rest period is allowed between the first and second games and a 10 minute rest period between the second and third games.

Players may leave the court between games, but must be on the court and rea
to play at the expiration of the rest period.

(e) **Postponed games.** Any games postponed by referee due to weather elements sh
be resumed with the same score as when postponed.

Part V. Tournaments

Rule 5.1   Draws. The seeding method of drawing shall be the standard method approv
by the U.S.R.A. and N.R.C. All draws in professional brackets shall be the responsibili
of the National Director of the N.R.C.

Rule 5.2   Scheduling (a) Preliminary matches. If one or more contestants are entered
both singles and doubles they may be required to play both singles and doubles on t
same day or night with little rest between matches. This is a risk assumed on enteri
both singles and doubles. If possible the schedule should provide at least a one hour r
period between all matches.

(b) **Final matches.** Where one or more players have reached the finals in both singl
and doubles, it is recommended that the doubles match be played on the d
preceding the singles. This would assume more rest between the final matche
If both final matches must be played on the same day or night, the following pr
cedure shall be followed:

(1) The singles match be played first.

(2) A rest period of not less than ONE HOUR be allowed between the finals
singles and doubles.

Rule 5.3   Notice of matches. After the first round of matches, it is the responsibility
each player to check the posted schedules to determine the time and place of each su
sequent match. If any change is made in the schedule after posting, it shall be the du
of the committee or chairman to notify the players of the change.

Rule 5.4   Third place. In championship tournaments: national, state, district, etc.,
there is a playoff for third place), the loser in the semi-finals must play for third pla
or lose his ranking for the next year unless he is unable to compete because of injury
illness. See Rule 3.5 (d) (4).

Rule 5.5   U.S.R.A. regional tournaments. Each year the United States and Canada a
divided into regions for the purpose of sectional competition preceding the Natior
Championships. The exact boundaries of each region are dependent on the location of t
regional tournaments. Such locations are announced in *National Racquetball* magazir

(a) Only players residing in the area defined can participate in a regional tournamer

(b) Players can participate in only one event in a regional tournament.

(c) Winners of open singles in regional tournaments will receive round trip air coa
tickets to the U.S.R.A. national tourney. Remuneration will be made after arriv
at the Nationals.

(d) A U.S.R.A. officer will be in attendance at each regional tournament and w
coordinate with the host chairman.

Awards: No individual award in U.S.R.A.-sanctioned tournaments should exceed val
of more than $25.

Tournament management: In all U.S.R.A.-sanctioned tournaments the tourname
chairman and/or the national U.S.R.A. official in attendance may decide on a chan
of courts after the completion of any tournament game if such a change will accommoda
better spectator conditions.

Tournament conduct: In all U.S.R.A.-sanctioned tournaments the referee is empower
to default a match if an individual player or team conducts itself to the detriment of t
tournament and the game.

Professional definition: Any player who has accepted $200 or more in prizes and/or pri
money in the most recent 12 calendar months is considered a professional racquetb
player and ineligible for participation in any U.S.R.A. sanctioned tournament bracke

Amateur definition: We hold as eligible for amateur racquetball tournaments sanctioned by the U.S.R.A. anyone except those who qualify as professionals under current U.S.R.A.-N.R.C. rules.

Pick-a-partner: The essence of the "Players' Fraternity" has been to allow players to come to tournaments and select a partner, if necessary, regardless what organization or city he might represent.

Age brackets: The following age brackets, determined by the age of the player on the first day of the tournament are:

Open: Any age can compete.

Juniors: 18 and under.

Seniors: 35 and over.

Masters: 45 and over.

Golden Masters: 55 and over.

In doubles both players must be within the specified age bracket.

One-wall and three-wall rules

Basically racquetball rules for one-wall, three-wall and four-wall are the same with the following exceptions:

One-wall—Court size Wall shall be 20 ft. in width and 16 ft. high, floor 20 ft. in width and 34 ft. from the wall to back edge of the long line. There should be a minimum of 3 feet beyond the long line and 6 feet outside each side line. There should be minimum of six feet outside each side line and behind the long line to permit movement area for the players.

Short line Back edge 16 feet from the wall. Service Markers—Lines at least 6 inches long parallel to and mid-way between the long and short lines, extending in from the side lines. The imaginary extension and joining of these lines indicates the service line. Lines are 1½ inches in width. Service Zone—floor area inside and including the short side and service lines. Receiving Zone—floor area in back of short line bounded by and including the long and side lines.

Three-wall—serve A serve that goes beyond the side walls on the fly is player or side out. A serve that goes beyond the long line on a fly but within the side walls is the same as a "short."

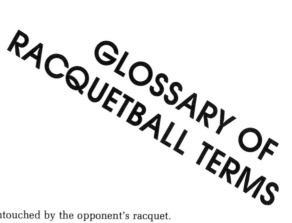
Ace   A legal serve that is untouched by the opponent's racquet.

Around-the-wall shot   A defensive shot that hits a side wall, then the front wall, then the other side wall before touching the floor.

Avoidable hinder   An interference with the opponent's play that could have been prevented or avoided.

Back court   The last 15 feet of the court, covering the area from the receiving line to the back wall.

Back-wall shot   A shot made on a ball rebounding off the rear wall.

Backswing   The portion of the swing when the racquet is brought back in preparation for hitting the ball.

Ceiling shot   A shot that hits the ceiling before hitting the front wall.

Center court   The area of the court just behind the short line, midway between the side walls.

Crotch shot   A shot that hits the juncture of any two playing surfaces.

Cross-court pass shot   A shot that is hit from one side of the court and, after hitting the front wall, travels to the opposite side of the court out of reach of the opponent.

Cutthroat   A game involving three players in which the server plays against the other two players.

Dead ball   A ball that is no longer in play.

Defensive shot   A shot which is made in order to continue a rally, in an attempt to maneuver an opponent out of the center court position.

Doubles   A game or match in which a team (consisting of two players) opposes another team.

Down-the-line shot   A shot hit near a side wall which hits the front wall directly, then rebounds back along the same side wall.

Drive   A powerfully hit ball that travels in a straight line.

Drop shot   A shot that is hit with very little force and rebounds only a few feet from the front wall.

Fault   An illegal serve, or an infraction of the rules, while serving. Two faults result in a side out.

Follow-through   The continuation of the swing after contact is made with the ball.

Foot fault   An illegal position in which the server's foot is outside the service zone during the serve.

Front court   The first 15 feet of the court from the front wall to the service line.

Front-wall kill   A kill shot that hits and rebounds off the front wall, touches neither side walls, and returns so that the opponent is unable to retrieve it.

Game   The portion of a match which is completed when one player, or team, reaches 21 points.

Garbage serve   A half lob hit halfway up the front wall which rebounds to the receiver at about shoulder height.

Garfinkel serve   A cross-court serve which hits the front, then the side wall, and bounds to the opponent's forehand.

Half and half   (Also called *side by side*.) A method of player positioning when playing doubles. Each player covers half of the court, either the left or right side.

Half volley   To hit the ball on the rise, just after it bounces on the floor. The shot resulting from this action.

Hand-out   Loss of the serve.

Hinder   An unintentional interference or screen of the ball so that the opponent does not have a fair chance to make a return. The point is replayed, without penalty.

I formation   (Also called *up and back*.) A method of player positioning used for doubles. One player covers the front court, the other the back court.

Inning   A round of play which is completed after both teams have served.

I.R.A.   International Racquetball Association.

Kill shot   An offensive shot which hits the front wall so low that a return by the opponent is impossible.

Lob shot   A shot hit high and gently toward the front wall, which rebounds to the back wall in a high arc.

Long serve   A serve that rebounds to the back wall without hitting the floor. This is a fault.

Match   A period of play which ends when one player, or team, wins two out of three games.

Mid court   The area of the court between the service line and the receiving line.

N.R.C.   National Racquetball Club. Oversees professional racquetball competition.

Offensive shot   An aggressive shot designed to win the point as fast as possible.

Overhead   A shot hit at shoulder level, or higher.

Passing shot   A shot hit past an opponent, out of his reach.

Pinch shot   A kill shot that hits the side wall, then the front wall.

Plum   A ball that can be easily killed.

Point   A unit used in scoring. It can only be won by the serving team.

Rally   An exchange of shots which is continued until play ends.

Ready position   A stance which is taken by a player while waiting for a serve or shot.

Receiving line   A mark on the side wall at a point five feet behind the short line.

Roll-Out   A shot in which the ball rolls out on the floor after rebounding off the front wall. A sure point, since it is impossible to retrieve.

Safety hinder   A situation in which play is stopped in order to prevent a player from being injured.

Screen   An interference with the opponent's vision of the ball.

Serve   The act of putting the ball into play; the shot which is used to accomplish this.

Service line   The front line of the service zone.

Service zone   The area between the service line and short line.

Setup   A shot that can be easily returned. *See* Plum.

Shooter   A player who tries to kill the ball.

Short line   The back line of the service zone. It is located at the midpoint of the court.

Short serve   A serve that fails to pass the short line. This is a fault.

Side by side   *See* Half and half.

Side out   The loss of serve to the opponent.

Singles   A racquetball game in which one player opposes another player.

Skip ball   A low ball that hits the floor before reaching the front wall.

Straight kill   *See* Front-wall kill.

Three-wall serve   A serve that hits two walls plus the front wall. This is a fault.

Throat   The part of the racquet between the strings and the grip.

Up and back   *See* I formation.

U.S.R.A.   United States Racquetball Association. The amateur organization within the N.R.C.

V shot   A shot where the ball hits the front wall, then rebounds off the side wall near the short line. The ball rebounds behind the opponent.

Volley   To hit the ball before it bounces. The shot resulting from this action.

Wallpaper shot A shot hit so close to the side wall that it is difficult to return.

Z serve Same as Z shot, except the ball hits the floor before hitting the third wall.

Z shot A ball which is hit high into the front wall corner, rebounds to the near side wa then to the opposite side wall.

BIBLIOGRAPHY

BOOKS

Fleming, A. William and Bloom, Joel A. *Paddleball and Racquetball.* Pacific Palisades, Calif.: Goodyear, 1973.

Keeley, Steve. *The Complete Book of Racquetball.* Northfield, Ill.: DBI Books, 1976.

Leve, Chuck. *Inside Racquetball.* Chicago: Regnery, 1973.

Rich, Jim. *Fundamentals of Racquetball.* Dubuque, Iowa: Kendall-Hunt, 1975.

Shay, Arthur with Leve, Chuck. *Winning Racquetball.* Chicago: Regnery, 1976.

Stafford, Randy. *Racquetball: The Sport For Everyone.* Memphis, Tenn.: S.C. Toof, 1975.

Wickstrom, Ralph and Larson, Charles. *Racquetball and Paddleball.* Columbus, Ohio: Merrill, 1972.

MAGAZINES

National Racquetball, 4101 Dempster Street, Skokie, IL 60076.

Racquetball, P.O. Box 1016, Stillwater, OK 74074.

3